T0190226

IoT Projects with NVIDIA Jetson Nano

AI-Enabled Internet of Things Projects for Beginners

Agus Kurniawan

Apress®

IoT Projects with NVIDIA Jetson Nano: AI-Enabled Internet of Things Projects for Beginners

Agus Kurniawan
Faculty of Computer Science, Universitas Indonesia, Depok, Indonesia

ISBN-13 (pbk): 978-1-4842-6451-5   ISBN-13 (electronic): 978-1-4842-6452-2
https://doi.org/10.1007/978-1-4842-6452-2

Copyright © 2021 by Agus Kurniawan

This work is subject to copyright. All rights are reserved by the publisher, whether the whole or part of the material is concerned, specifically the rights of translation, reprinting, reuse of illustrations, recitation, broadcasting, reproduction on microfilms or in any other physical way, and transmission or information storage and retrieval, electronic adaptation, computer software, or by similar or dissimilar methodology now known or hereafter developed.

Trademarked names, logos, and images may appear in this book. Rather than use a trademark symbol with every occurrence of a trademarked name, logo, or image, we use the names, logos, and images only in an editorial fashion and to the benefit of the trademark owner, with no intention of infringement of the trademark.

The use in this publication of trade names, trademarks, service marks, and similar terms, even if they are not identified as such, is not to be taken as an expression of opinion as to whether or not they are subject to proprietary rights.

While the advice and information in this book are believed to be true and accurate at the date of publication, neither the authors nor the editors nor the publisher can accept any legal responsibility for any errors or omissions that may be made. The publisher makes no warranty, express or implied, with respect to the material contained herein.

Managing Director, Apress Media LLC: Welmoed Spahr
Acquisitions Editor: Natalie Pao
Development Editor: James Markham
Coordinating Editor: Jessica Vakili

Distributed to the book trade worldwide by Springer Science+Business Media New York, 1 NY Plaza, New York, NY 10014. Phone 1-800-SPRINGER, fax (201) 348-4505, email orders-ny@springer-sbm.com, or visit www.springeronline.com. Apress Media, LLC is a California LLC and the sole member (owner) is Springer Science+Business Media Finance Inc (SSBM Finance Inc). SSBM Finance Inc is a **Delaware** corporation.

For information on translations, please e-mail booktranslations@springernature.com; for reprint, paperback, or audio rights, please e-mail bookpermissions@springernature.com.

Apress titles may be purchased in bulk for academic, corporate, or promotional use. eBook versions and licenses are also available for most titles. For more information, reference our Print and eBook Bulk Sales web page at http://www.apress.com/bulk-sales.

Any source code or other supplementary material referenced by the author in this book is available to readers on GitHub via the book's product page, located at www.apress.com/978-1-4842-6451-5. For more detailed information, please visit http://www.apress.com/source-code.

Printed on acid-free paper

Table of Contents

About the Author

Agus Kurniawan is a lecturer, IT consultant, and author. He has fifteen years of experience in various software and hardware development projects, delivering materials in training and workshops, and technical writing. He has been awarded the Microsoft Most Valuable Professional (MVP) award fifteen years in a row.

Agus is a lecturer and researcher in the field of networking and security systems at the Faculty of Computer Science, Universitas Indonesia, Indonesia. Currently, he is pursuing a PhD in computer science at the Freie Universität in Berlin, Germany. He can be reached on Twitter at @agusk2010.

About the Technical Reviewer

Sai Yamanoor is an embedded systems engineer working for an industrial gases company in Buffalo, New York. His interests, deeply rooted in DIY and open source hardware, include developing gadgets that aid behavior modification. He has published two books with his brother, and in his spare time he likes to contribute to building things that improve quality of life. You can find his project portfolio at `http://saiyamanoor.com`.

CHAPTER 1

Introduction to NVIDIA Jetson Nano

NVIDIA Jetson Nano is an NVIDIA product that can implement IoT solutions with the power of GPU computation. This board has GPIO pins and a GPU core to help developers, makers, and IT users build programs easily. In this chapter, we will get a brief introduction to NVIDIA Jetson Nano.

We will cover the following topics:

- Introduction to NVIDIA Jetson Nano

- Exploration of technical specifications of NVIDIA Jetson Nano

- Exploration of NVIDIA Jetson Nano's functionalities

Introduction

The Nvidia Jetson Nano was announced as a development system in mid-March of 2019. This product is intended for Internet of Things (IoT) makers. The board consists of a CPU with 1.43 GHz and a GPU with 128 cores of the Maxwell generation.

The first model of NVIDIA Jetson that was released for the consumer public can be seen in Figure 1-1. It's called NVIDIA Jetson Nano A02.

© Agus Kurniawan 2021
A. Kurniawan, *IoT Projects with NVIDIA Jetson Nano*,
https://doi.org/10.1007/978-1-4842-6452-2_1

Now, NVIDIA has releasee a new model, the NVIDIA Jetson Nano B01. Technically, both models have the same CPU and GPU, but some peripherals are changed. You can see the NVIDIA Jetson Nano B01 in Figure 1-2. In this chapter, we will review the specifications of the NVIDIA Jetson Nano.

Figure 1-1. *NVIDIA Jetson Nano A02*

Figure 1-2. *NVIDIA Jetson Nano B01*

NVIDIA Jetson Nano Hardware Specifications

In general, NVIDIA Jetson Nano has the technical specifications shown in Table 1-1. You can see it has a GPU with 128 cores. This feature is useful if you want to perform high computation on this machine.

Table 1-1. *NVIDIA Jetson Nano Features*

Feature	Information
GPU	128-core Maxwell
CPU	Quad-core ARM A57 @ 1.43 GHz
Memory	4 GB 64-bit LPDDR4 25.6 GB/s
Storage	microSD
Video Encode	4K @ 30 | 4x 1080p @ 30 | 9x 720p @ 30 (H.264/H.265)
Video Decode	4K @ 60 | 2x 4K @ 30 | 8x 1080p @ 30 | 18x 720p @ 30 (H.264/H.265)
Camera	2x MIPI CSI-2 DPHY lanes
Connectivity	Gigabit Ethernet, M.2 Key E
Display	HDMI and display port
USB	4x USB 3.0, USB 2.0 Micro-B
I/O	GPIO, I2C, I2S, SPI, UART
Mechanical	69 mm x 45 mm, 260-pin edge connector

To obtain an NVIDIA Jetson Nano board, you can visit the official website at https://developer.nvidia.com/buy-jetson?product=jetson_nano. You can see NVIDIA distributors that sell NVIDIA Jetson Nano.

You can also obtain this board at your local electronic store. You could probably find it on online stores such as SparkFun or SeeedStudio.

What Can We Do with NVIDIA Jetson Nano?

NVIDIA Jetson Nano is designed for general purposes to address computer problems. Let's see what we can do.

Daily Computer Activities

We can say the NVIDIA Jetson Nano is a computer of small size. Since NVIDIA Jetson Nano is a computer, we can treat it as an everyday computer. We can browse the internet to look for information.

We also can use it for daily computer activities such as writing documents, creating spreadsheets, and printing documents. We can install office applications from LibreOffice. By default, LibreOffice is already included in the NVIDIA Jetson Nano image. You can see my LibreOffice application in Figure 1-3.

The user must just provide a keyboard, mouse, and monitor so as to make their own personal computer. It's useful to apply for teaching on classroom or computer lab activities.

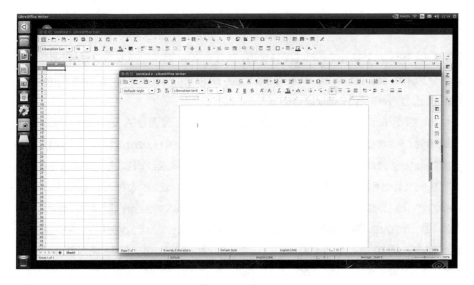

Figure 1-3. *Running LibreOffice application on NVIDIA Jetson Nano*

Internet of Things Development

The primary goal for NVIDIA Jetson Nano is to build IoT solutions. We can add sensor and actuator modules to NVIDIA Jetson Nano devices. The board provides a GPIO interface so as to be attached to external device modules.

Other I/O interfaces such as serial communication, SPI, and I2C can be accessed from our program. This board can leverage your IoT business and projects.

Programming platforms like C/C++ and Python are supported in the NVIDIA Jetson Nano image. Since this image uses operating system–based Ubuntu, we can install various compilers and applications, including web applications and databases.

We will explore these features, IoT, and software applications in Chapters 4 and 5.

AI Development

NVIDIA Jetson Nano has a GPU with 128 cores. This resource can be used for AI applications. We can run Pandas, Numpy, Tensorflow, and Keras on an NVIDIA Jetson Nano board.

We only focus on how to build AI programs. NVIDIA Jetson Nano will take over your computations. To obtain optimized computation, make sure your library and program support GPU cores from NVIDIA Jetson Nano.

If you have interest in computer vision, you can apply NVIDIA Jetson Nano to do that. You can attach external cameras via the CSI interface or USB camera. By installing the *OpenCV* library, we can utilize NVIDIA Jetson Nano to create great computer vision programs. OpenCV library provides various image and video processing libraries. We can use it on your programs such as C/C++ and Python directly. In addition, OpenCV consists of machine learning libraries like face recognition.

We will explore AI computation on NVIDIA Jetson Nano in Chapters 6 and 7.

Summary

We have explored what NVIDIA Jetson Nano is. We also learned what one does with it.

Next, we will learn how to set up NVIDIA Jetson Nano in order to get started with this board.

CHAPTER 2

Setting Up and Running

This chapter explores how to set up NVIDIA Jetson Nano in order to run the system. We can install and configure all software on the NVIDIA Jetson Nano device.

We will cover the following topics:

- Preparing hardware
- Setting up software
- Running NVIDIA Jetson Nano
- Configuring NVIDIA Jetson Nano software
- Working with Terminal
- Restarting and shutting down

Introduction

NVIDIA Jetson Nano can be treated as a mini computer. You will need some hardware and software stuff, such as mouse, keyboard, and monitor.

© Agus Kurniawan 2021
A. Kurniawan, *IoT Projects with NVIDIA Jetson Nano*,
https://doi.org/10.1007/978-1-4842-6452-2_2

Hardware Preparation

We prepare some hardware for NVIDIA Jetson Nano on this section. Since this board does not have internal storage, you need external storage. The board only supports a microSD card for internal storage. This storage device will be used to store the operating system (OS) and data. You probably need a microSD card reader to enable you to work with your computer to read and write files. Figure 2-1 shows my NVIDIA Jetson Nano, microSD card, and microSD card reader.

Figure 2-1. *MicroSD card and NVIDIA Jetson Nano*

In general, you'll need some additional hardware to run your NVIDIA Jetson Nano device. The following are required additional devices:

- MicroSD card with 16 GB storage size minimum

- MicroSD card reader to write and read files from a computer

- Mouse with USB wired

- Keyboard with USB wired

- Power adapter 5V 2A

- Micro USB cable for power adapter

- Monitor with HDMI connector

You can find these items at local and online stores. Some electronics stores also provide an NVIDIA Jetson Nano package that contains all required hardware to set up the NVIDIA Jetson Nano system environment.

After you complete the hardware requirements, you can prepare the software needed to get the NVIDIA Jetson Nano running. We will set up the software in the next section.

Set Up Software

The NVIDIA Jetson Nano uses its own OS to run its applications. This OS is based on Ubuntu Linux. If you have experience with Ubuntu Linux, you can perform any Ubuntu activity on an NVIDIA Jetson Nano.

You can download the Jetson Nano Developer Kit SD Card Image from `https://developer.nvidia.com/jetson-nano-sd-card-image`. You will get a ZIP file for the image file.

Next, you will need to flash the NVIDIA image file onto the microSD card. Depending on your OS platform, you can do so using some tools, such as SD Memory Card Formatter for Windows.

For this demo, we use the Etcher tool to flash the NVIDIA image file onto a microSD card. This tool is available for Windows, Linux, and macOS. You can see the form of the Etcher tool in Figure 2-2.

Plug your microSD card with reader into your computer. Now you are ready to flash the NVIDIA Jetson Nano image.

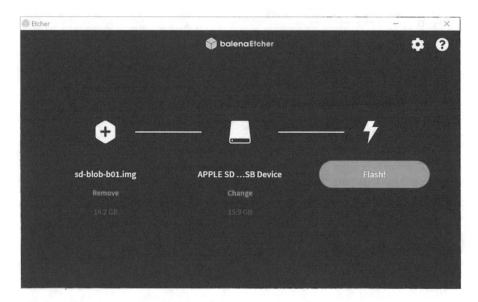

Figure 2-2. *Etcher application*

You can start to flash the image file by selecting *image file*. Select *NVIDIA image file (ZIP file)*. Then, select your microSD card. If your microSD card is not recognized by your OS, you can format your microSD card with FAT mode. File Allocation Table (FAT) usualy is used in a personal computer with Windows OS.

Now you can start to flash the NVIDIA Jetson Nano image onto your microSD card. Click the *Flash!* button. You will be asked to give administrator permission to flash the image. This process takes a few minutes to complete.

You will get confirmation after completing the flashing. Figure 2-3 shows a completion of flashing image with the Etcher application.

You can unplug your microSD card from your computer if you have finished flashing the image file. Then, you can put it on the NVIDIA Jetson Nano device.

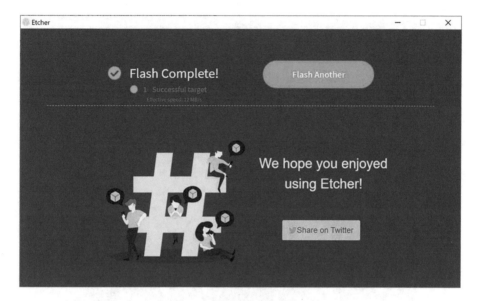

Figure 2-3. *Flashing Jetson Nano Developer Kit SD card image*

Run NVIDIA Jetson Nano

In this section, we will run NVIDIA Jetson Nano for the first time. After you have flashed the NVIDIA Jetson Nano image onto the microSD card, you can attach the card to the NVIDIA Jetson Nano board. You can put it on the back of the processor module. Figure 2-4 shows an attached microSD card on an NVIDIA Jetson Nano.

You can plug the keyboard, mouse, and monitor into the NVIDIA Jetson Nano device. To power the NVIDIA Jetson Nano device, you can use DC jack power or micro USB power. In my case, I use micro USB power with power adapter 5V, 2A. You can see my configuration in Figure 2-5. I also attached a keyboard and mouse to the board.

If you use a power adapter on the DC jack, please make sure you use a jumper on the Power Select Header from NVIDIA Jetson Nano.

After you have plugged all your peripherals into the NVIDIA Jetson Nano device, you will get a confirmation page. You will be asked to configure your board. We will configure NVIDIA Jetson Nano in the next section.

Figure 2-4. *Plugging microSD card into NVIDIA Jetson Nano device*

Figure 2-5. *Plug in keyboard, mouse, monitor, and power adapter*

Configure NVIDIA Jetson Nano Software

After you've plugged in a power adapter, you can configure the NVIDIA Jetson Nano for the first time. There are some settings that you should complete; use the keyboard and mouse.

First, you get a form for agreement as shown in Figure 2-6. You should accept this agreement if you want to continue to use the NVIDIA Jetson Nano device. Click the *Continue* button.

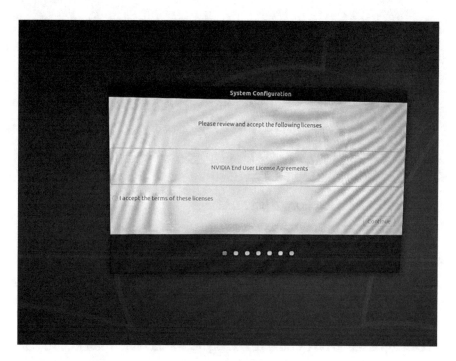

Figure 2-6. *User agreement on NVIDIA Jetson Nano*

Furthermore, you will be asked to select a language for all text on the NVIDIA Jetson Nano. You also can set keyboard type and time zone for local region. Last, create your account for the NVIDIA Jetson Nano. Enter full name, username, and password, as shown in Figure 2-7. Also, set the authentication model. It's recommended you use the *Require my password to log in* option.

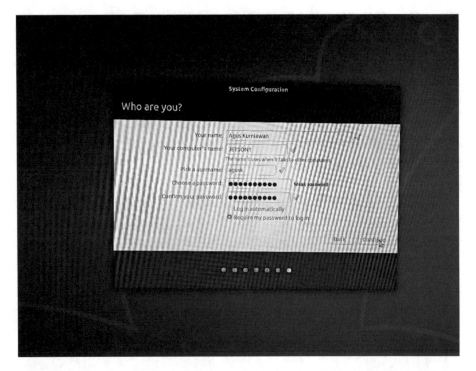

Figure 2-7. *Creating a new account*

If your NVIDIA Jetson Nano is connected to the internet through a LAN cable or Wi-Fi module, you can connect to the internet. Then, you can update the NVIDIA Jetson Nano software. We will discuss the NVIDIA Jetson Nano network in the next chapter.

After completing all tasks, you will see the NVIDIA Jetson Nano desktop. This desktop is based on Ubuntu Linux. Figure 2-8 shows the desktop. You can perform normal activities as you would on any computer, such as creating and editing files, browsing the internet, chatting, and so forth.

Figure 2-8. *NVIDIA Jetson Nano desktop*

Terminal

Since the NVIDIA Jetson Nano image is built from Ubuntu, you can use Terminal to perform administration tasks, such as creating/editing files and folders or compiling and executing programs. Mostly, people perform Linux administration with Terminal.

You can find NVIDIA Jetson's Terminal by clicking Search on the top left. Type "Terminal" so you can see the Terminal application, as shown in Figure 2-9. After clicking the Terminal icon, you will get the Terminal application, as shown in Figure 2-10.

For a demo, you can type this command in Terminal. You will get Linux information inside the board.

```
uname -a
```

Press the *Enter* key after typing that command. The following is a program output from the umane -a command.

Linux JETSON1 4.9.140-tegra #1 SMP PREEMPT Thu Jun 25 21:25:44 PDT 2020 aarch64 aarch64 aarch64 GNU/Linux

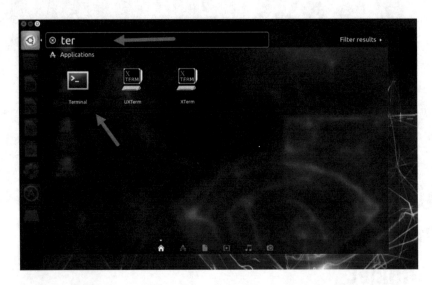

Figure 2-9. *Opening Terminal on NVIDIA Jetson Nano*

Figure 2-10. *Terminal application*

If you want to close the Terminal application, you can type this command:

```
exit
```

Now you can perform administration tasks using Terminal. We will learn more on this topic in the next chapter.

Restart and Shut Down

Sometimes you want to reboot your NVIDIA Jetson Nano OS after completing system configurations. You can reboot it manually. You can click the Settings icon at the top right of the NVIDIA Jetson Nano desktop. You will get a menu, as shown in Figure 2-11. Select *Shut Down* from the menu.

After doing so, you will get a confirmation dialog, as shown in Figure 2-12. There are two options: *Shut Down* and *Restart*. Select *Restart* to reboot the NVIDIA Jetson Nano.

You can also reboot NVIDIA Jetson Nano via Terminal. You can open Terminal by pressing the *CTRL* and *T* keys simultaneously. After opening Terminal, you can type this command:

```
sudo reboot
```

The NVIDIA Jetson Nano device will reboot automatically. Make sure you save all data before you perform a reboot.

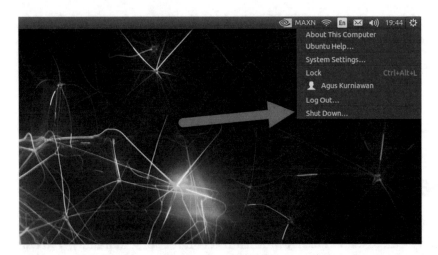

Figure 2-11. *Opening a menu for Shut Down*

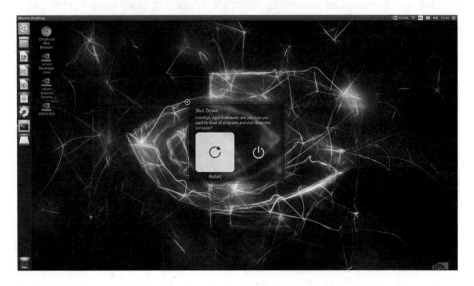

Figure 2-12. *A confirmation dialog for reboot and shut down*

If you don't need to use the NVIDIA Jetson Nano anymore, you can shut it down. You can do this in the same way as you did the restart task. You just select the *Shut Down* option on the confirmation dialog (Figure 2-12).

You also can perform a shutdown using Terminal. You can type this command:

```
shutdown
```

This command will shut down the NVIDIA Jetson Nano by scheduling. It usually takes one minute. If you want to shut down the board without scheduling, you can use the shutdown command with parameter -P. You can type this command in Terminal:

```
sudo shutdown -P now
```

The now parameter means we shut down the NVIDIA Jetson Nano immediately after executing this command.

Practice by working on the NVIDIA Jetson Nano desktop.

Summary

You have learned how to prepare hardware and software for the NVIDIA Jetson Nano device. We installed the Jetson Nano Developer Kit SD Card Image into a microSD card. Then, we ran and configured the NVIDIA Jetson Nano.

Next, we will continue to work with the NVIDIA Jetson Nano. We will administer the OS on NVIDIA Jetson Nano for basic administration.

CHAPTER 3

Administering NVIDIA Jetson Nano

The NVIDIA Jetson Nano device is a mini computer with high-end features and GPU capabilities. The board system consists of hardware and software. In this chapter, you will learn to manage the NVIDIA Jetson Nano with administration software.

You will learn some basics of device administration, such as the following:

- Desktop personalization

- Terminal

- Managing users

- Connecting a network through Ethernet and Wi-Fi

- Browsing the internet

- Office administration

- SSH and SFTP

- Update package repository

- Remote desktop

© Agus Kurniawan 2021
A. Kurniawan, *IoT Projects with NVIDIA Jetson Nano*,
https://doi.org/10.1007/978-1-4842-6452-2_3

Introduction

The NVIDIA Jetson Nano system consists of both hardware and software. The software is built from Ubuntu Linux. In this chapter, we will explore how to manage the NVIDIA Jetson Nano software. You can perform Linux administration tasks on the NVIDIA Jetson Nano device. We don't cover all Linux administration tasks, but rather focus on essential ones that enable you to manage and address issues on your NVIDIA Jetson Nano device.

Desktop Personalization

The NVIDIA Jetson Nano software uses the Ubuntu desktop as its platform. After completed to run NVIDIA Jetson Nano, you will obtain an Ubuntu desktop. You can customize this desktop with different themes and wallpaper. You can perform this task through the Appearance window, as shown in Figure 3-1. You can find this tool in *Settings*.

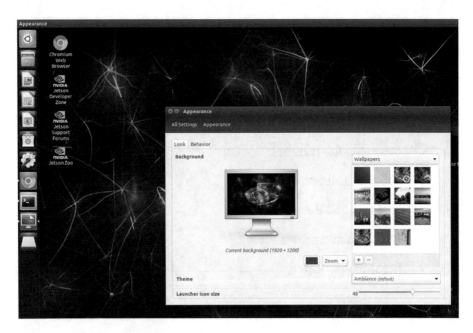

Figure 3-1. *Customizing NVIDI Jetson Nano desktop*

Working with Terminal

In the previous chapter, we learned how to get started with Terminal. Now, you can manage your NVIDIA Jetson Nano via Terminal. You can open Terminal by pressing *CTRL + T*. It will look as shown in Figure 3-2.

Figure 3-2. *Terminal on NVIDIA Jetson Nano*

Some basic NVIDIA Jetson Nano Terminal commands include the following:

- pwd

- ls

- cd

- mkdir & rmdir & rm

- touch

- sudo

- cp

- mv

- which

We will explore these Linux commands in the next section.

pwd

You can find out the current directory that you are working in using the pwd command. You can type it in Terminal as follows:

```
pwd
```

Then, you can see your current directory. This is a sample output from the pwd command:

```
$ pwd
/home/agusk
```

ls

The ls command is used to list the files and directories found in the current folder. For instance, you can type this command:

```
$ ls
Desktop Documents Downloads examples.desktop jetson-inference
Music Pictures Public Templates Videos
```

You can also set the -l parameter on the ls command to get the details of the listing result. You can see the following sample of the ls -l command:

```
$ ls -l
total 48
drwxr-xr-x  2 agusk agusk 4096 Jul 27 12:17 Desktop
drwxr-xr-x  2 agusk agusk 4096 Jul 27 12:17 Documents
drwxr-xr-x  2 agusk agusk 4096 Jul 27 12:17 Downloads
-rw-r--r--  1 agusk agusk 8980 Jul 27 12:15 examples.desktop
drwxrwxr-x 13 agusk agusk 4096 Jul 27 12:53 jetson-inference
drwxr-xr-x  2 agusk agusk 4096 Jul 27 12:17 Music
drwxr-xr-x  2 agusk agusk 4096 Jul 28 11:49 Pictures
drwxr-xr-x  2 agusk agusk 4096 Jul 27 12:17 Public
drwxr-xr-x  2 agusk agusk 4096 Jul 27 12:17 Templates
drwxr-xr-x  2 agusk agusk 4096 Jul 27 12:17 Videos
```

So far, we have performed the ls command on the current directory.
You can specify a target directory as well. For instance, if you want to see a
list of the files and directories found in the /var/log folder:

```
$ ls /var/log
alternatives.log    btmp         installer        syslog     Xorg.0.log
alternatives.log.1  btmp.1       kern.log         syslog.1   Xorg.0.log.old
apt                 dpkg.log     kern.log.1       tallylog   Xorg.1.log
auth.log            dpkg.log.1   lastlog          wtmp       Xorg.1.log.old
auth.log.1          gdm3         oem-config.log   wtmp.1
```

cd

This command, cd, is used to change the current directory to another directory. For a demo, we will navigate to the Document folder from the current home directory.

```
$ pwd
/home/agusk
$ cd Documents/
~/Documents$ pwd
/home/agusk/Documents
```

mkdir and rmdir

The mkdir command is used to create a directory. The rmdir command is used to delete an empty directory. The following is a program sample:

```
$ ls
$ mkdir myfolder
$ ls
myfolder
$ rmdir myfolder/
$ ls
$
```

If you delete a directory that consists of files or directories using rmdir, you will get an error. For instance, if you tried to delete the test folder, which contains a file, you would see the following error message:

```
$ rmdir test/
rmdir: failed to remove 'test/': Directory not empty
```

rm

If you want to delete a directory, including its contents, you can use the rm command with the -r parameter. For instance, if you wanted to delete the test folder and its contents, you'd use the following:

```
rm -r test/
```

touch

The touch command allows you to create a new blank file. You can type these commands to try it out:

```
$ touch data
$ ls
data
```

sudo

This command enables you to perform tasks that require administrative or root permissions. However, please don't use sudo to perform just any task, due to security issues. For instance, if you wanted to create a folder with the sudo command, you'd type the following:

```
$ sudo mkdir hello
```

After you executed the command above, you will see a folder, hello, in current folder where you are running this command

cp

You can use the cp command to copy a file from a certain directory to another directory. If you don't specify a path, sit will just use the current directory. For demo, we want to copy a file on /var/log/auth.log to current directory. We can use dot (.) for current directory with the same file name.

```
$ ls
data
$ cp /var/log/auth.log .
$ ls
auth.log   data
```

mv

The mv command is used to move files. This command can also be used to rename files. For instance, if you wanted to rename a *data* file to be called *newdata* in the current directory, you would type these commands:

```
$ ls
auth.log   data
$ mv data newdata
$ ls
auth.log   newdata
```

which

The which command is used to give the full path location of a program. For instance, if you wanted to know a location of the Python program, you'd type the following:

```
$ which python3
/usr/bin/python3
```

Managing Users

During the initial system configuration process, you must create a new account. You can add additional user accounts on the NVIDIA Jetson Nano device. You can achieve this task with the desktop GUI and Terminal. We will explore these methods in the next section.

Managing Users with GUI

You can create a new user account on the NVIDIA Jetson Nano to allow that user to access the system. Open the User Account pane from *Settings*. The User Account pane is shown in Figure 3-3.

Figure 3-3. *A user account*

To add a new account, click the *Unlock* button at the top right. Then, you'll see a dialog for administrator permission. Enter the administrator password. After that, add or remove users by clicking the + and – icons.

If you click the + icon you will see the dialog shown in Figure 3-4. Select Account Type and fill in Full Name and Username. Click the *Add* button if you are finished.

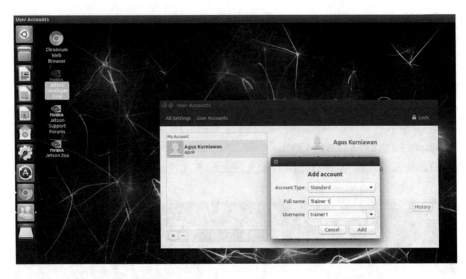

Figure 3-4. *Adding a new account*

Now you can see the new account on the list. By default, the new account is disabled. Figure 3-5 shows that the new account, Trainer 1, has *disabled* status.

Figure 3-5. *A new account on User Accounts pane*

To activate this account, click the *Account disabled* button. Then, you will see the dialog shown in Figure 3-6. Select an action for this account; for instance, *Set a password now*. Then, you can enter a password for this account.

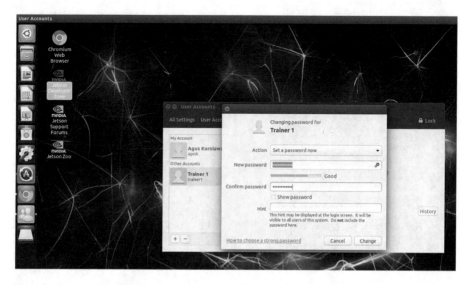

Figure 3-6. *Enabling user account by applying password*

You can delete a user account from the NVIDIA Jetson Nano. From the account list on the User Account pane (Figure 3-5), select the account you want to delete and then select the – icon to remove the selected account.

Next, we will see how to manage accounts from the NVIDIA Jetson Nano Terminal.

Managing Users with Terminal

Ubuntu Linux on the NVIDIA Jetson Nano provides the option to manage users using Terminal. You can use the adduser command to create a new account. For instance, you can type this command in Terminal:

```
sudo adduser <account>
```

Change <account> to your new account. After that, you will be asked to fill in the password and user information, as shown in Figure 3-7.

```
agusk@JETSON1: ~                                               —    □    X
agusk@JETSON1:~$ agusk@JETSON1:~$
agusk@JETSON1:~$ sudo adduser trainer2
[sudo] password for agusk:
Adding user `trainer2' ...
Adding new group `trainer2' (1002) ...
Adding new user `trainer2' (1002) with group `trainer2' ...
Creating home directory `/home/trainer2' ...
Copying files from `/etc/skel' ...
Enter new UNIX password:
Retype new UNIX password:
passwd: password updated successfully
Changing the user information for trainer2
Enter the new value, or press ENTER for the default
        Full Name []: Trainer 2
        Room Number []:
        Work Phone []:
        Home Phone []:
        Other []:
Is the information correct? [Y/n] y
Adding new user `trainer2' to extra groups ...
Adding user `trainer2' to group `audio' ...
Adding user `trainer2' to group `crypto' ...
Adding user `trainer2' to group `gdm' ...
Adding user `trainer2' to group `gpio' ...
Adding user `trainer2' to group `i2c' ...
Adding user `trainer2' to group `trusty' ...
Adding user `trainer2' to group `video' ...
Adding user `trainer2' to group `weston-launch' ...
agusk@JETSON1:~$
```

Figure 3-7. *Adding a new account with Terminal*

You can delete a user by using the deluser command. For instance, if you wanted to remove the trainer2 username, you would type this command:

sudo deluser trainer2

However, you can also delete a username, including its home directory, with the −remove-home parameter in the deluser command. For instance, if you wanted to delete the trainer2 account and its home directory, you'd type the following:

sudo deluser --remove-home trainer2

Connecting to a Network

The NVIDIA Jetson Nano device has a built-in network module with Ethernet. We can plug a LAN cable into the Ethernet port on an NVIDIA Jetson Nano. Figure 3-8 shows my NVIDIA Jetson Nano device with a plugged-in UTP LAN cable. Once the NVIDIA Jetson Nano device is connected to a network, you can verify its IP address using the ifconfig command in Terminal.

```
ifconfig
```

You will see the IP address of your NVIDIA Jetson Nano.

Figure 3-8. *Connecting a UTP LAN cable to a NVIDIA Jetson Nano*

If you do not see the IP address, your network probably does not have a DHCP server. However, you can configure a static IP address on the NVIDIA Jetson Nano using Terminal. You can modify a file in /etc/network/interfaces. Use the nano program. If your NVIDIA Jetson Nano does not have this program, you can install it as follows:

```
sudo apt-get install nano
```

Now, you can modify a file in /etc/network/interfaces using nano, as follows:

```
sudo nano /etc/network/interfaces
```

Then, you can write a static IP address. For instance, if you wanted to set your IP address to be 192.168.1.10 and gateway IP address to be 192.168.1.1, you could write these scripts in the /etc/network/interfaces file:

```
iface eth0 inet static
address 192.168.1.10
netmask 255.255.255.0
gateway 192.168.1.1
```

Save the file. Now NVIDIA Jetson Nano has a static IP address.

Connecting to Wi-Fi Network

The NVIDIA Jetson Nano doesn't come with built-in Wi-Fi, so you need an additional device if you want to access a Wi-Fi network. There are two options: you can use a Wi-Fi module or a Wi-Fi USB dongle. We will explore these options in the next sections.

Wi-Fi Network Card Module

The NVIDIA Jetson Nano provides an e-connector to enable you to attach your Wi-Fi network card to the board. You can use Intel Dual Band Wireless-Ac 8265 w/Bluetooth 8265.NGWMG on NVIDIA Jetson Nano.

To attach the Wi-Fi network card, you should open the NVIDIA module from the board. Then, put the Wi-Fi network card into the connector. You can see my installation in Figure 3-9.

Figure 3-9. Attaching Wi-Fi module into NVIDIA Jetson Nano

Now you can see a list of Wi-Fi SSIDs on your desktop. You can select a Wi-Fi SSID and enter the SSID key if it's available.

After connecting to the internet over Wi-Fi, you can access resources such as browsing the internet, accessing files over the network, and sending emails via the browser.

Wi-Fi USB Dongle

You can use a Wi-Fi USB dongle on the NVIDIA Jetson Nano to access a Wi-Fi network. Technically, you can use any Wi-Fi USB dongle model, but your Wi-Fi USB dongle has a device driver.

I have tested Netgear and Belkin Wi-Fi USB dongle devices on my NVIDIA Jetson Nano. These devices are supported without installing a driver. Just plug in the dongle to the USB connector. Then you can use this device immediately.

Figure 3-10 shows my Netgear Wi-Fi USB dongle connected to an NVIDIA Jetson Nano. You can connect a Wi-Fi SSID from the Wi-FI SSID list. Enter the SSID key if the Wi-Fi SSD requires authentication.

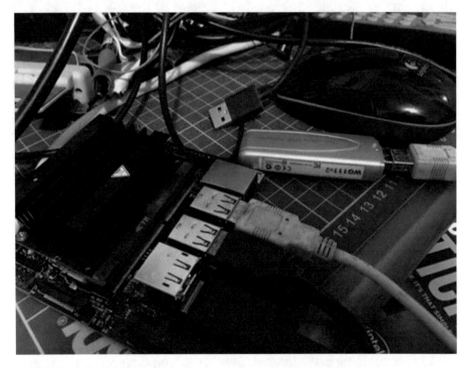

Figure 3-10. Plugging in Wi-Fi USB to NVIDIA Jetson Nano

Browsing the Internet

NVIDIA Jetson Nano comes with an installed Chromium browser. You can use this browser to surf the internet or to just open and send email. Figure 3-11 shows the Chromium browser accessing a website. You can find the Chromium shortcut link on the NVIDIA Jetson Nano device. Click the Chromium icon on the desktop to open the Chromium application.

Figure 3-11. *Browsing internet with Chromium*

If you prefer to use another browser such as FireFox or Chrome, you can install it manually on NVIDIA Jetson Nano. You can download Firefox, Chrome, or Opera through the Chromium browser.

For instance, you can download Firefox from https://www.mozilla. org/en-US/firefox/new. Download and install this browser on your NVIDIA Jetson Nano. You also can install Firefox using Terminal. Type this command:

```
sudo apt install firefox
```

You will get the Firefox browser on your device. Now you can surf the internet with your favorite browser.

Office Administration

NVIDIA Jetson Nano isn't only intended for specific purposes; anyone can use this board for daily computer activities such as writing and printing documents.

You can find LibreOffice on NVIDIA Jetson Nano's desktop. You can write documents and perform data manipulation with Spreadsheet. Figure 3-12 shows the LibreOffice application.

If you have a printer device, you can attach it to your NVIDIA Jetson Nano. You can register that printer. Then, you print documents through the LibreOffice application.

Figure 3-12. *LibreOffice on NVIDIA Jetson Nano*

SSH

NVIDIA Jetson Nano can be managed remotely. You can use SSH to remote access the board. An SSH server has been installed on the NVIDIA Jetson Nano. You can use your SSH client application to access NVIDIA Jetson Nano.

For instance, you can use PuTTY on Windows to access the SSH server. You can download this tool from `https://www.putty.org`. You can see the PuTTY application in Figure 3-13. You just enter the IP address of the NVIDIA Jetson Nano. Set the SSH option on PuTTY. If finished, you can click the *Open* button.

After connecting to the NVIDIA Jetson Nano, you will be challenged for security. Enter the username and password for your registered account on the NVIDIA Jetson Nano. If it succeeds, you will see Terminal, as shown in Figure 3-14.

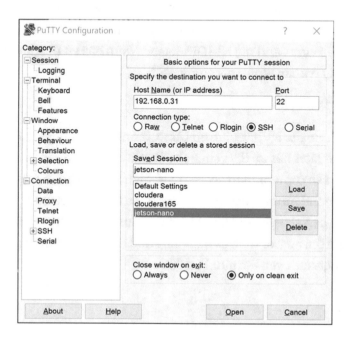

Figure 3-13. *Accessing SSH using PuTTY in Windows*

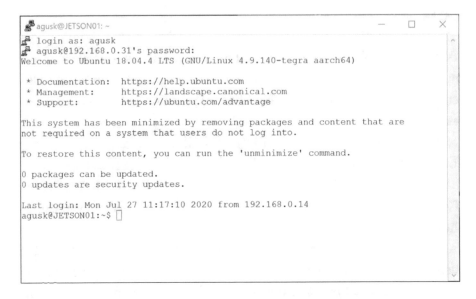

Figure 3-14. *Accessing NVIDIA Jetson Nano using PuTTY*

If you are working with Linux or macOS, you can access the NVIDIA Jetson Nano using the ssh command on Terminal. For instance, I use agusk as username, and my NVIDIA Jetson Nano has an IP address of 192.168.0.31. We can write this command:

```
ssh agusk@192.168.0.31
```

You will see the NVIDIA Jetson Nano Terminal. Windows 10 Update April 2018 or later has an SSH client built into the command prompt. You can use the ssh command to access SSH. Figure 3-15 shows the SSH client in the command prompt being used to access NVIDIA Jetson Nano.

Now we can access the NVIDIA Jetson Nano remotely over SSH. We can manage the board, such as installing and updating libraries. We also can run programs over Terminal on SSH.

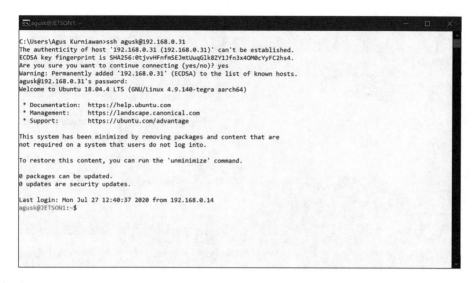

Figure 3-15. *SSH client on Windows 10 Command prompt*

Access Remote Files over SFTP

We can download and transfer files to the NVIDIA Jetson Nano using SFTP. This is useful when you want to upload programs to the NVIDIA Jetson Nano.

We can use SFTP client with the FileZilla application. This tool is available for Windows, macOS, and Linux. You can download this tool at `https://filezilla-project.org`.

After downloading the FileZilla application, you can open this tool. Add a new site and then set the IP address of your NVIDIA Jetson Nano. Select SFTP for the protocol. Fill in your username and password. Figure 3-16 shows the FileZilla application for the Windows platform.

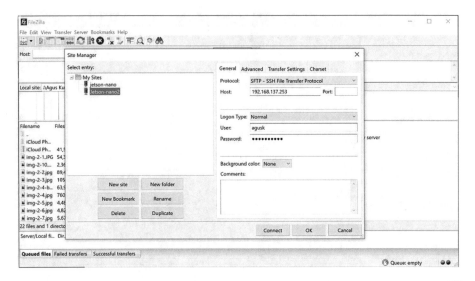

Figure 3-16. *SFTP client with FileZilla application*

Click the *Connect* button if you have filled in the IP address and account information for the NVIDIA Jetson Nano. You can then see your home directory from your account. Figure 3-17 shows FileZilla accessing the NVIDIA Jetson Nano device over the SFTP network.

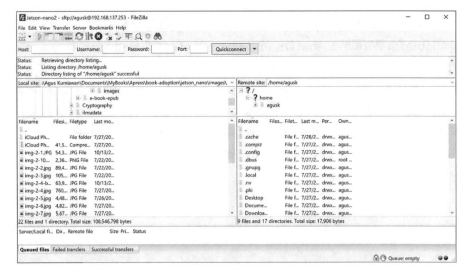

Figure 3-17. *Accessing SFTP on NVIDIA Jetson Nano*

Now you can download and upload files to your NVIDIA Jetson Nano using FileZilla. You can also create, edit, and delete directories.

Update Package Repository

Some libraries on the NVIDIA Jetson Nano device are probably outdated, so you should update your package repository. You can perform this task in Terminal by typing this command:

```
sudo apt-get update
```

Make sure your NVIDIA Jetson Nano device is connected to the internet. The repository list is updated. You can upgrade all applications using the following command:

```
sudo apt-get upgrade
```

Remote Desktop

Sometimes you want to remote your NVIDIA Jetson Nano board from your computer. We can use remote desktop application. You can utilize the remote desktop functionality on the NVIDIA Jetson Nano using the nano server. This library is already installed on the NVIDIA Jetson Nano image. To run nano server, you should log in to the NVIDIA Jetson Nano desktop. Then, open Terminal. Type this command:

```
$ /usr/lib/vino/vino-server
```

Now a nano server is running. You can see my nano server is running in Figure 3-18. Next, you can open the VNC client application to access the NVIDIA Jetson Nano desktop remotely.

Figure 3-18. *Running vino-server NVIDIA Jetson Nano desktop*

For this demo, I use the VNC Viewer application as the VNC client. You can download this tool at https://www.realvnc.com/. Create a new connection and enter the IP address of the NVIDIA Jetson Nano. Click the *OK* button when finished. Figure 3-19 shows the VNC Viewer application.

If we could connect to the NVIDIA Jetson Nano device, we would see a confirmation dialog, as shown in Figure 3-20. Click the *Continue* button to access the NVIDIA Jetson Nano desktop.

If you obtain an error due to an encryption issue while connecting to the NVIDIA Jetson Nano desktop, you can use require-encryption. You can open Terminal and type this command:

```
gsettings set org.gnome.Vino require-encryption false
```

Now, you can run the nino server again on the NVIDIA Jetson Nano. After that, you can open the VNC client application.

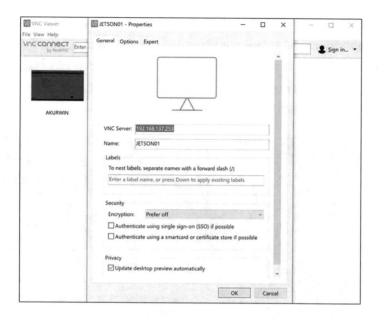

Figure 3-19. *Setting up VNC viewer for NVIDIA Jetson Nano*

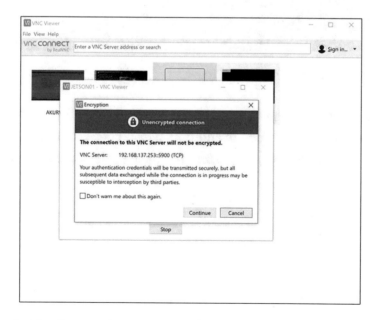

Figure 3-20. *Connecting a remote desktop on NVIDIA Jetson Nano*

When you try to connect to NVIDIA Jetson Nano over remote desktop, you will obtain a connection confirmation, as shown in Figure 3-21. Click the *Accept* button if you want to allow for performing remote desktop. After this is accepted, you can obtain theNVIDIA Jetson Nano desktop in VNC viewer application, as shown in Figure 3-22.

Figure 3-21. *Giving approval to access NVIDIA Jetson Nano desktop*

If you are still getting an error, please check the IP Address of NVIDIA Jetson Nano is correct or not. In addition, please check your network router you that it allows to access remote desktop with a certain port.

Figure 3-22. *NVIDIA Jetson Nano desktop is connected from VNC client*

This is the end of the chapter. You should practice administering NVIDIA Jetson Nano device.

Summary

We have learned how to administer the NVIDIA Jetson Nano device. We used Terminal to manage our system. We also connected the NVIDIA Jetson Nano device to the internet network using Ethernet and a Wi-Fi module. We explored how to access the NVIDIA Jetson Nano device remotely using VNC viewer, SSH, and SFTP.

Next, we will learn how to write programs for the NVIDIA Jetson Nano device.

CHAPTER 4

NVIDIA Jetson Nano Programming

The NVIDIA Jetson Nano device is designed for developers who want to build programs on the board. In this chapter, we will explore how to build programs on the NVIDIA Jetson Nano. We will review some compilers and interpreters included in the development tools.

In this chapter, we will learn about the following:

- Editor tools

- C/C++ programs

- Python programs

- Node.js programs

Next, we will explore editor tools used to write code on the NVIDIA Jetson Nano device.

Introduction

The NVIDIA Jetson Nano device image is built from Ubuntu Linux. To build programs on the NVIDIA Jetson Nano device, we should consider all program constraints of a Linux-based platform. Technically, we should use a Linux-based programming approach if we want to build programs on this board.

© Agus Kurniawan 2021
A. Kurniawan, *IoT Projects with NVIDIA Jetson Nano*,
https://doi.org/10.1007/978-1-4842-6452-2_4

All program models will be explained in this chapter. We will discuss a common program language that we will probably use in our project. We will explore some programs in the next section.

Editor Tools

To write programs on the NVIDIA Jetson Nano device, you need a text editor. You can use an official editor from the Ubuntu desktop, such as gedit. However, you also can use vi and nano to write code. You can install nano using this command on Terminal:

```
sudo apt-get install nano
```

This command will download the nano program to the repository server and then install it on your NVIDIA Jetson Nano. Make sure your board is connected to the internet.

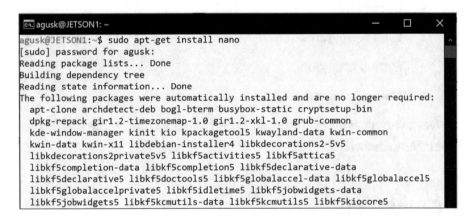

Figure 4-1. *Installing nano program on NVIDIA Jetson Nano*

Figure 4-1 shows a nano installation through the NVIDIA Jetson Nano Terminal. Make sure your board is connected to the internet.

Now you can create a new file with nano. For instance, to create a file, *hello.sh*, you can type this command:

```
nano hello.sh
```

Now, obtain the nano editor via Terminal, as shown in Figure 4-2. For this demo, we will write these scripts with nano editor. The program will print "Hello World!!" in Terminal.

```
#!/bin/sh

echo Hello World!!
```

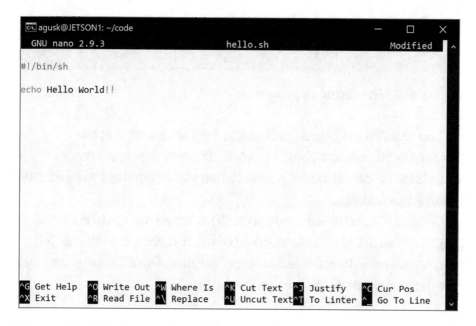

Figure 4-2. *Writing codes using nano editor*

Save these scripts. Now you can run this program. First, change the script file to be an executable file using the chmod 755 command. Then, call ./hello to run the program:

```
chmod 755 hello.sh
./hello
```

After executing this program, you will see the program output, as shown in Figure 4-3.

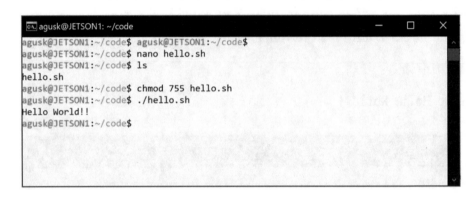

Figure 4-3. *Executing sh program*

You can also use Visual Studio Code from Microsoft. You can find further information about Visual Studio Code at https://code. visualstudio.com. This tool is useful when you're working on the NVIDIA Jetson Nano desktop.

To install Visual Studio Code on NVIDIA Jetson Nano, use the Code program from https://code.headmelted.com. Build Visual Studio Code from source code. Install this tool using Terminal. Open Terminal and then type these commands (please don't write $).

```
$ sudo -s
$ . <( wget -O - https://code.headmelted.com/installers/apt.sh
)
```

First, enter administrator mode by calling sudo -s. This command will download and build the source code of Visual Studio Code. This process will take several minutes. After finishing this process, you can exit administrator mode by typing exit in Terminal:

```
exit
```

Now you can head back to the NVIDIA Jetson Nano desktop. Open the main menu and search by typing "code." You will see Code - OSS (Headmelted) as shown in Figure 4-4.

Figure 4-4. *Visual Studio Code shortcut on main menu*

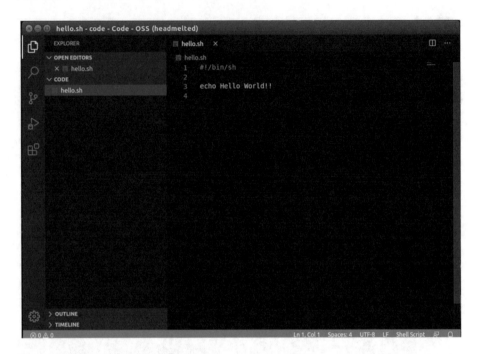

Figure 4-5. *Visual Studio Code*

You can open this tool and open a file or folder. For instance, you can open the *hello.sh* file, as shown in Figure 4-5.

C/C++

You can build programs for C/C++ on your NVIDIA Jetson Nano. The NVIDIA Jetson Nano image includes GCC compiler, so you can use that for compiling C/C++. To verify your GCC version, open Terminal and type this command:

```
gcc --version
```

You should see the GCC version in Terminal. Figure 4-6 shows my GCC version on my NVIDIA Jetson Nano.

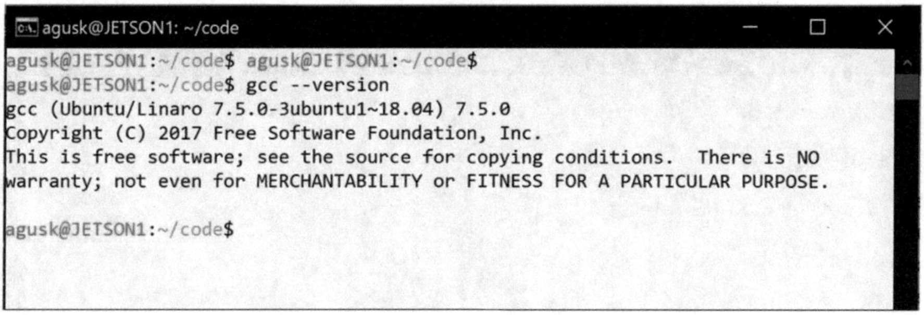

```
agusk@JETSON1: ~/code                                    —    □    ×
agusk@JETSON1:~/code$ agusk@JETSON1:~/code$
agusk@JETSON1:~/code$ gcc --version
gcc (Ubuntu/Linaro 7.5.0-3ubuntu1~18.04) 7.5.0
Copyright (C) 2017 Free Software Foundation, Inc.
This is free software; see the source for copying conditions.  There is NO
warranty; not even for MERCHANTABILITY or FITNESS FOR A PARTICULAR PURPOSE.

agusk@JETSON1:~/code$
```

Figure 4-6. *Checking GCC version*

For this demo, you will write a simple C program, using nano as the editor tool. Create a file, *helloc.c.* In this program, you will show the text "Hello World\n" in Terminal. \n indicates a new line, so after the program shows "Hello World" the cursor will move on to the new line.

Write this code for implementation in the nano editor tool:

```c
#include<stdio.h>

int main()
{
    printf("Hello World\n");
    return 0;
}
```

Save this code. Figure 4-7 shows the code for the *helloc.c* file.

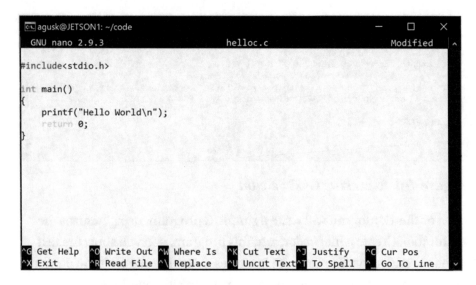

Figure 4-7. *Writing C code using nano*

Now you can compile and run this program. In Terminal, call gcc and then run the program as follows:

```
gcc hello.c -o helloc
./helloc
```

After execution, you should see the text "Hello World" in Terminal. Figure 4-8 shows the compiled and executed program from the *helloc.c* file.

This is a sample program to show how to get started with C programming on the NVIDIA Jetson Nano. For C++ code, you can use GCC or G++ to compile C++ code.

What's next? You can dive deep to explore building C/C++ programs on your NVIDIA Jetson Nano. You could use learning resources for C/C++ to start to write C/C++ codes.

```
agusk@JETSON1: ~/code                                    —    □    ×
agusk@JETSON1:~/code$ agusk@JETSON1:~/code$
agusk@JETSON1:~/code$ ls
helloc.c   hello.sh
agusk@JETSON1:~/code$ gcc helloc.c -o helloc
agusk@JETSON1:~/code$ ./hello
helloc     hello.sh
agusk@JETSON1:~/code$ ./helloc
Hello World
agusk@JETSON1:~/code$
```

Figure 4-8. *Compiling and executing C program*

Python

Python is a scripting programming that most developers use to build data processing and data science implementations. Python can also be used to build hardware programming. There are various Python libraries that provide hardware drive interfaces.

In this section, we will learn how to get started with Python programming on NVIDIA Jetson Nano devices. Python 2.7 and Python 3.x are installed by default via the NVIDIA Jetson Nano image. You can verify this by typing this command in Terminal:

```
python --version
```

You should see Python 2.7.x listed in Terminal. For Python 3.x, you can use the python3 command, as follows:

```
python3 --version
```

Now you can use the Python shell so you can write Python scripts and then get the output directly. In this demo, we will use the Python 3 shell. Type this command in Terminal:

```
python3
```

After execution, you should see the Python shell and see >>> in Terminal, as shown in Figure 4-9. Inside the Python shell >>>, you write these scripts:

```
>>> a = 10
>>> b = 5
>>> c = a * b
>>> c
```

After you type this and press the *Enter* key, you should obtain output from the Python shell, as shown in Figure 4-9.

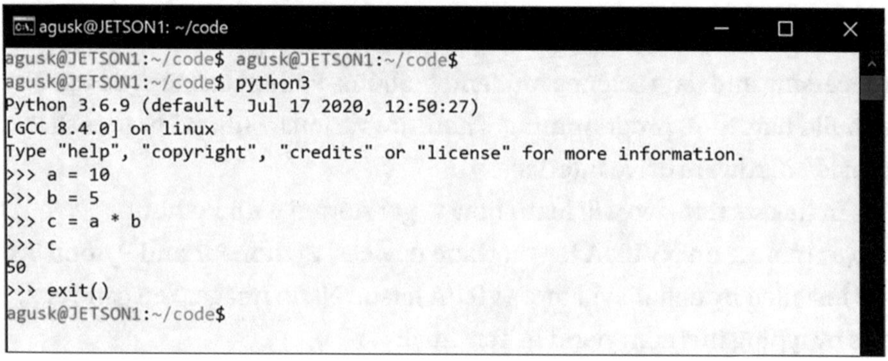

```
agusk@JETSON1: ~/code                                    —    □    ×
agusk@JETSON1:~/code$ agusk@JETSON1:~/code$
agusk@JETSON1:~/code$ python3
Python 3.6.9 (default, Jul 17 2020, 12:50:27)
[GCC 8.4.0] on linux
Type "help", "copyright", "credits" or "license" for more information.
>>> a = 10
>>> b = 5
>>> c = a * b
>>> c
50
>>> exit()
agusk@JETSON1:~/code$
```

Figure 4-9. *Running Python shell*

When working on data processing or data science, most developers use Jupyter Notebook, https://jupyter.org, to write and run Python scripts. You can install Jupyter Notebook on your NVIDIA Jetson Nano. Open Terminal and then type these commands:

```
sudo apt-get install python3-pip
sudo pip3 install jupyter
```

It takes several minutes to download and install Jupyter Notebook. Make sure your NVIDIA Jetson Nano is connected to the internet. After completing the installation, you can run Jupyter Notebook by typing this command in Terminal:

```
jupyter notebook
```

If you run this command on the NVIDIA Jetson Nano desktop, you will get a browser that shows the Jupyter Notebook application, as shown in Figure 4-10.

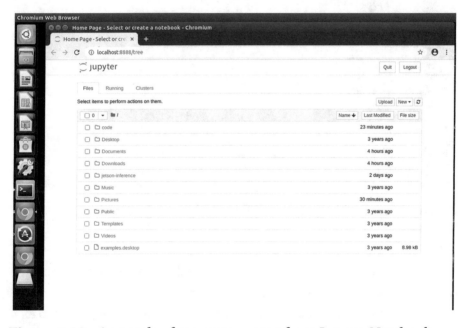

Figure 4-10. *A sample of program output from Jupyter Notebook*

To create a new notebook, click the *New* dropdown on the right-hand menu. Select *Python 3*. Then, you'll see a notebook, as shown in Figure 4-11. Write this Python script for demo practice:

```
a = 10
b = 7
```

```
c = a * b
c
```

You can run this code by clicking the *Run* icon. You should see program output from this code like that shown in Figure 4-11.

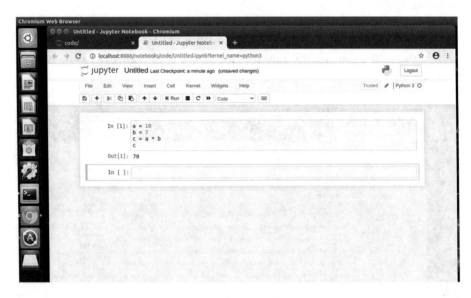

Figure 4-11. *Writing and executing Python script on Jupyter Notebook*

You can save this program by clicking the disk icon on the toolbar menu. You can also rename the file by clicking on *Title*.

What's next? You can learn more about Python programs. You can use nano, Visual Studio Code, or Jupyter Notebook to write Python scripts. Find public resources or Python documentation to learn the Python programming language.

Node.js

Node.js is a programming language based on JavaScript. It is cross-platform as it is intended to be general purpose. You can build web applications using Node.js.

To install Node.js on your NVIDIA Jetson Nano device, you can type this command:

```
sudo apt-get install nodejs npm
```

You get a node command for your Node.js application. You can check the node version by typing this command:

```
node --version
```

You will see the Node.js version on the NVIDIA Jetson Nano. Figure 4-12 shows my Node.js version on my NVIDIA Jetson Nano.

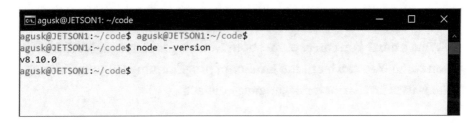

Figure 4-12. *Checking Node.js version*

For this demo, you will write a simple program. You can write Node.js code by creating a file, *hellojs.js*, in the nano tool. Write this code:

```
console.log("Hello Node.js");
```

You can see my Node.js code in nano in Figure 4-13.

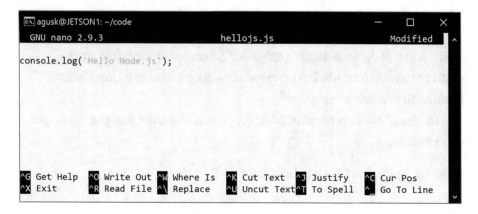

Figure 4-13. *Writing Node.js codes in nano*

Save this program. To run it, you can use the node command with the *Node.js* file as parameter. For instance, to run the *hellojs.js* file, type this command:

```
node hellojs.js
```

You should see text "Hello Node.js" on Terminal.

What's next? You can explore about Node.js programs on NVIDIA Jetson Nano. You can learn the JavaScript programming language, since Node.js uses JavaScript for its language dialect.

Summary

We learned how to write code on the NVIDIA Jetson Nano device. We reviewed editor tools to help you write code. We also have tried to write and run codes for C/C++, Python, and Node.js.

Next, we will learn how to do I/O programming on the NVIDIA Jetson Nano. We focus on GPIO hardware programming.

CHAPTER 5

NVIDIA Jetson Nano I/O Programming

Both the A02 and B01 models of the NVIDIA Jetson Nano have GPIO pins on the J41 header. We can thus extend some sensors and actuators into NVIDIA Jetson Nano devices. NVIDIA Jetson Nano also provides GPIO pins for UART, PWM, SPI, I2S, and I2C. In this chapter, we will explore GPIO programming on the NVIDIA Jetson Nano, including sensors and actuators.

You will learn about the following topics in this chapter:

- Setting up GPIO

- GPIO programming

- Sensor programming

- Actuator programming

You will need some peripherals in order to implement the demos in this chapter. We will explore more in the next section.

© Agus Kurniawan 2021
A. Kurniawan, *IoT Projects with NVIDIA Jetson Nano*,
https://doi.org/10.1007/978-1-4842-6452-2_5

Introduction

A general-purpose input/output (GPIO) is an uncommitted digital signal pin on a board. On NVIDIA Jetson Nano, you can find GPIO pins on the J41 header. You can see the pin layout of the NVIDIA Jetson Nano board in Figure 5-1, as indicated by the red arrow.

Figure 5-1. *GPIO pinout on NVIDIA Jetson Nano*

A detail of the GPIO pinout can be seen in Figure 5-2. You can see pins for GPIO, UART, SPI, I2S, and I2C.

The NVIDIA Jetson Nano GPIO can use from 1.8V to 3.3V. By default, all GPIO pins use 3.3V. Make sure you don't use a pin input voltage of more than 3.3V. Otherwise, your board will be broken.

Name	Pin	Pin	Name
3.3 VDC	1	2	5.0 VDC
I2C_2_SDA I2C Bus 1	3	4	5.0 VDC
I2C_2_SCL I2C Bus 1	5	6	GND
AUDIO_MCLK	7	8	UART_2_TX /dev/ttyTHS1
GND	9	10	UART_2_RX /dev/ttyTHS1
UART_2_RTS	11	12	I2S_4_SCLK
SPI_2_SCK	13	14	GND
LCD_TE	15	16	SPI_2_CS1
3.3 VDC	17	18	SPI_2_CS0
SPI_1_MOSI	19	20	GND
SPI_1_MISO	21	22	SPI_2_MISO
SPI_1_SCK	23	24	SPI_1_CS0
GND	25	26	SPI_1_CS1
I2C_1_SDA	27	28	I2C_1_SCL
CAM_AF_EN	29	30	GND
GPIO_PZ0	31	32	LCD_BL_PWM
GPIO_PE6	33	34	GND
I2S_4_LRCK	35	36	UART_2_CTS
SPI_2_MOSI	37	38	I2S_4_SDIN
GND	39	40	I2S_4_SDOUT

Figure 5-2. *GPIO pins on NVIDIA Jetson Nano*

Each GPIO pin can be used as an input pin or an output pin. The GPIO number labels are shown on the NVIDIA Jetson Nano board. The GPIO number is useful when you want to access GPIO on the NVIDIA Jetson Nano.

Setting Up GPIO

To access the NVIDIA Jetson Nano GPIO, use the *Jetson.GPIO* library from Jetson. This library is modified from the *RPI GPIO* (Raspberry Pi) library. You can build Python applications with *Jetson.GPIO* to access the NVIDIA Jetson Nano device. You can find the *Jetson.GPIO* library at `https://github.com/NVIDIA/jetson-gpio`.

Now you can install *Jetson.GPIO* on the NVIDIA Jetson Nano using `pip` from Python. Open Terminal and type this command:

```
$ sudo pip install Jetson.GPIO
```

If you use Python 3, you will probably use `pip3` to install NVIDIA Jetson Nano. Please make sure to use this `pip` program. Here is how to install *Jetson.GPIO* with the `pip3` program:

```
$ sudo pip3 install Jetson.GPIO
```

You need to configure security permission on the NVIDIA Jetson Nano in order to run your programs. Create a new `gpio` user group. Then, add your current account into this `gpio` group. Type these commands:

```
$ sudo groupadd -f -r gpio
$ sudo usermod -a -G gpio <your_account>
```

You also need to copy the *99-gpio.rules* file into the /etc/udev/rules.d/ folder. The *99-gpio.rules* file is usually available in /usr/local/lib/python3.6/dist-packages/. You can verify using this command (for Python 3, change python for Python 2.7.x):

```
$ python3 -m site
```

You should see a path of the dist-packages folder from Python. For instance, we have a path for the usr/local/lib/python3.6/dist-packages/ folder, so we can move the *99-gpio.rules* file into the /etc/udev/rules.d/ folder with the following command:

```
$ sudo cp /usr/local/lib/python3.6/dist-packages/Jetson/
GPIO/99-gpio.rules /etc/udev/rules.d/
```

After completing this installation, you can verify its success by opening Python shell. For instance, we use Python 3. Type these commands:

```
$ python3
>>> import Jetson.GPIO as GPIO
>>> GPIO.JETSON_INFO
>>> GPIO.VERSION
```

You should see the *Jetson.GPIO* library information and version. You can see my library information in Figure 5-3.

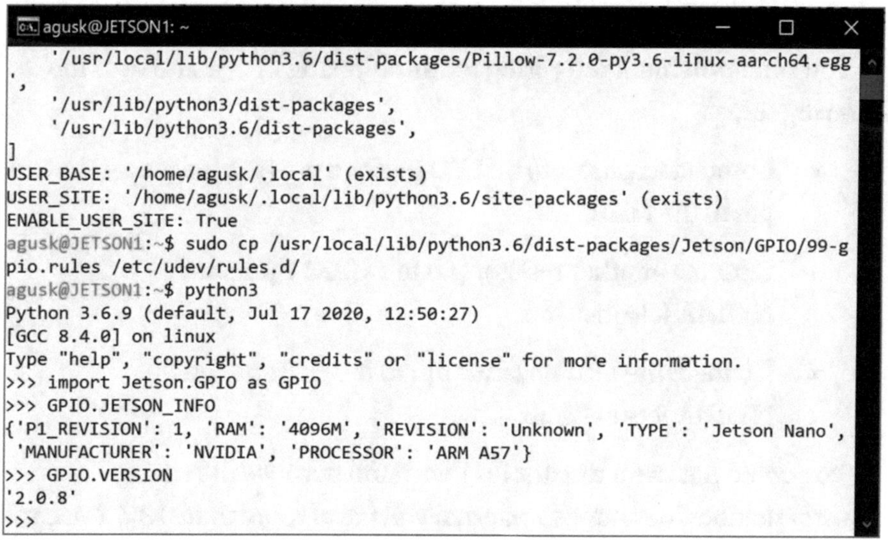

Figure 5-3. *Checking Jetson.GPIO version*

If you get any errors when checking the *Jetson.GPIO* version, you probably have problems in installation.

Now, we can build programs to access the NVIDIA Jetson Nano GPIO pins.

GPIO Programming

The NVIDIA Jetson Nano board has forty GPIO pins. You can see this in Figure 5-2. You can use a GPIO pin in either input mode or output mode. You can't use it in input and output modes simultaneously.

For this demo, you can use an LED and make it blink. You need the following electronic components:

- Breadboard

- LED

- A resistor; you can use 220 or 300 ohm

- Two jumper cables

You can implement the wiring for this blinking LED demo with the following steps:

- Connect a resistor to an LED positive pin (the longest pin of the LED).

- Connect another resistor pin to a GPIO 7 pin on the NVIDIA Jetson Nano.

- Connect the LED negative pin to the GND pin on the NVIDIA Jetson Nano.

You could not use a resistor for this demo because the wiring implementation does not use external voltage of more than 3.3V. You can see my wiring in Figure 5-4. I don't use a resistor for this demo.

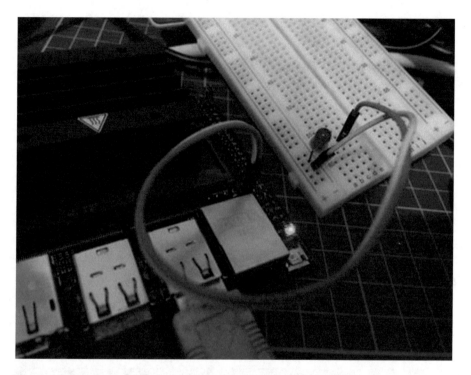

Figure 5-4. *Attaching an LED to the NVIDIA Jetson Nano*

Now you can write a program to turn the LED on and off. Open Terminal on the NVIDIA Jetson Nano. Then, create a file, *gpiodemo.py*, using nano. You probably could use any text editor to write the program script.

```
$ nano gpiodemo.py
```

After nano is open, write the following script:

```
import Jetson.GPIO as GPIO
import time

led_pin = 7
GPIO.setmode(GPIO.BOARD)
GPIO.setup(led_pin, GPIO.OUT)
```

```python
try:
    while 1:
        print("turn on led")
        GPIO.output(led_pin, GPIO.HIGH)
        time.sleep(2)
        print("turn off led")
        GPIO.output(led_pin, GPIO.LOW)
        time.sleep(2)

except KeyboardInterrupt:
    GPIO.output(led_pin, GPIO.LOW)
    GPIO.cleanup()

print("done")
```

Save this script into the file *gpiodemo.py*. You can see my program script in nano in Figure 5-5.

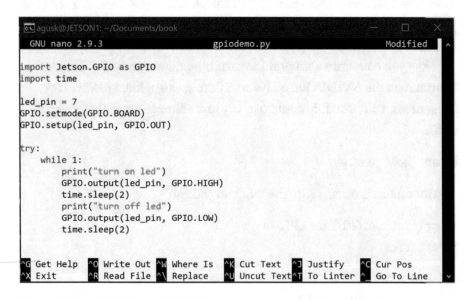

Figure 5-5. *Writing a GPIO program*

You can run your program, *gpiodemo.py*, in Terminal. You can use Python to run this Python program. Open Terminal and type this command:

```
$ python3 gpiodemo.py
```

If you get any errors due to security issues, you can run the *gpiodemo. py* file with the sudo command. Type this command:

```
$ sudo python3 gpiodemo.py
```

You should see blinking on the LED. You can also see the program output in Terminal. Figure 5-6 shows my program output for the *gpiodemo. py* program.

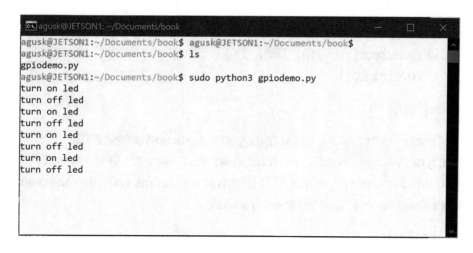

Figure 5-6. *Executing gpiodemo program*

How does it work?

This program starts with loading *Jetson.GPIO* and time modules.

```
import Jetson.GPIO as GPIO
import time
```

Then, it initializes a GPIO pin on the NVIDIA Jetson Nano. It declares led_pin for pin 7 with the GPIO.BOARD model. This model uses the GPIO pin number based on the board numbering. The program sets pin 7 as GPIO.OUT mode.

```
led_pin = 7
GPIO.setmode(GPIO.BOARD)
GPIO.setup(led_pin, GPIO.OUT)
```

To prevent errors, the program implements try...except to catch errors in the code. If there are errors, you can set your LED to off by calling GPIO.output(led_pin, GPIO.LOW). Then, release all resources in use.

```
try:

except KeyboardInterrupt:
    GPIO.output(led_pin, GPIO.LOW)
    GPIO.cleanup()

print("done")
```

Inside the try...except scripts, you turn on and off the LED. To turn it on, you set the GPIO.HIGH value on pin 7 using the GPIO.output() function. In these scripts, the LED is turned on and then off. Also, the code sets a delay for two seconds at each action.

```
    while 1:
        print("turn on led")
        GPIO.output(led_pin, GPIO.HIGH)
        time.sleep(2)
        print("turn off led")
        GPIO.output(led_pin, GPIO.LOW)
        time.sleep(2)
```

Now you can practice using some LEDs with GPIO pins on the NVIDIA Jetson Nano board. You can use any GPIO pin on the board.

Next, we will develop sensor devices on the NVIDIA Jetson Nano board.

Sensor Programming

You can attach various sensor modules to the NVIDIA Jetson Nano, but not all sensor interfaces are supported by it. You can use the following supported interface protocols on the NVIDIA Jetson Nano:

- Digital I/O

- UART (Serial Communication)

- SPI (Serial Peripheral Interface)

- I2C (Inter-Integrated Circuit)

- I2S (Inter-IC Sound Bus)

As we know, the NVIDIA Jetson Nano does not support analog I/O. This means if you plan to use sensor module-based analog I/O, you should use an additional module such as an ADC (Analog-to-Digital Converter) module that will convert analog sensor data to digital data so the NVIDIA Jetson Nano can process it.

For this demo, use a sensor module–based I2C interface. The I2C interface uses the device address so NVIDIA Jetson Nano can access data by opening a connection to the I2C address. Each analog sensor from the sensor module-based I2C will be attached to the I2C address.

For testing, I used a PCF8591 AD/DA converter module with sensor and actuator devices. This sensor module can be seen in Figure 5-7. The PCF8591 AD/DA module uses a PCF8591 chip that consists of four analog inputs and an AD converter. The PCF8591 chip also has analog output with a DA converter. Further information about the PCF8591 chip can be found sat https://www.nxp.com/products/interfaces/ic-spi-serial-interface-devices/ic-dacs-and-adcs/8-bit-a-d-and-d-a-converter:PCF8591.

Figure 5-7. *PCF8591 AD/DA converter module*

You can find it on online stores like Aliexpress. You could probably obtain this module at your local store.

Based on the datasheet documentation for the PCF8591 AD/DA converter module, we know this module uses I2C address on 0x48. The module also consists of three sensors, as follows:

- Thermistor. Using channel 0

- Photoresistor. Using channel 1.

- Potentiometer. Using channel 3.

The I2C interface has two pins: SDA and SCL. For data transfer, it uses the SDA pin. The SCL pin is used for clocking. Now attach the PCF8591 AD/DA converter module to your NVIDIA Jetson Nano with the following wiring:

- PCF8591 AD/DA module SDA is connected to NVIDIA Jetson Nano SDA pin 3

- PCF8591 AD/DA module SCL is connected to NVIDIA Jetson Nano SCL pin 5.

- PCF8591 AD/DA module VCC is connected to NVIDIA Jetson Nano 3.3V pin.

- PCF8591 AD/DA module GND is connected to NVIDIA Jetson Nano SDA GND pin.

You can see my wiring in Figure 5-8.

Figure 5-8. *PCF8591 AD/DA converter module connected to NVIDIA Jetson Nano*

Now you can detect the I2C address on the PCF8591 AD/DA converter module using the i2cdetect command. This tool is already installed on the NVIDI Jetson Nano image. You can type this command:

```
$ i2cdetect -y -r 1
```

After executing this command, you should see the I2C address from the PCF8591 AD/DA converter module. For instance, you can see my I2C address is 48 in Figure 5-9. The I2C address shows the value in hex format. It means my I2C address is 0x48.

Next, build a Python program to read the data from the PCF8591 AD/DA converter module. You will read Thermistor, Photoresistor, and Potentiometer data from this module.

```
agusk@JETSON1: ~/Documents/book                                    —    □    ×
agusk@JETSON1:~/Documents/book$ agusk@JETSON1:~/Documents/book$
agusk@JETSON1:~/Documents/book$ i2cdetect -y -r 1
     0  1  2  3  4  5  6  7  8  9  a  b  c  d  e  f
00:          -- -- -- -- -- -- -- -- -- -- -- -- --
10: -- -- -- -- -- -- -- -- -- -- -- -- -- -- -- --
20: -- -- -- -- -- -- -- -- -- -- -- -- -- -- -- --
30: -- -- -- -- -- -- -- -- -- -- -- -- -- -- -- --
40: -- -- -- -- -- -- -- -- 48 -- -- -- -- -- -- --
50: -- -- -- -- -- -- -- -- -- -- -- -- -- -- -- --
60: -- -- -- -- -- -- -- -- -- -- -- -- -- -- -- --
70: -- -- -- -- -- -- -- --
agusk@JETSON1:~/Documents/book$
```

Figure 5-9. *Checking I2C module address*

To access the I2C module, use the *smbus* library. By default, it is already installed on the NVIDIA Jetson Nano, but you can install it manually using this command:

```
$ sudo apt-get install python3-smbus
```

Now write the Python program for reading the sensor data. You can use any editor. Write this complete Python program to read sensor data from PCF8591 AD/DA converter module:

```
import time, math
import smbus

bus = smbus.SMBus(1)
```

```python
address = 0x48

def photo():
    val = bus.read_i2c_block_data(address,1,2)
    return val

def potentiometer():
    val = bus.read_i2c_block_data(address,3,2)
    return val

def thermistor():
    val = bus.read_i2c_block_data(address,0,2)
    return val

try:
    while 1:
        val = thermistor()
        print('thermistor: ',val[1])
        time.sleep(1)

        val = photo()
        print('photo: ',val[1])
        time.sleep(1)

        val = potentiometer()
        print('potentiometer: ',val[1])
        time.sleep(1)

except KeyboardInterrupt:
    pass

print("done")
```

Save this program as *sensor.py*. Then, you can run this program in the NVIDIA Jetson Nano Terminal. You can open Terminal and navigate to the directory where the *sensor.py* file is placed. Type this command to execute the sensor program:

```
$ sudo python3 sensor.py
```

After execution, you should see sensor data. Figure 5-10 shows my program output from the *sensor.py* application.

How does it work?

This program starts by loading the I2C module using smbus. It also loads the time and math modules.

```
import time, math
import smbus
```

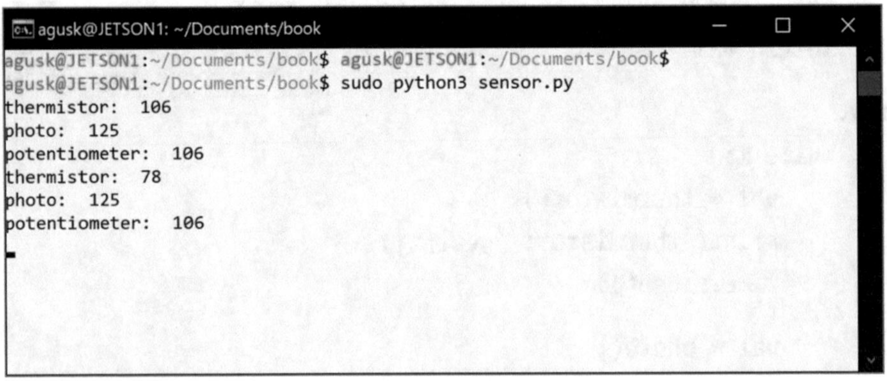

Figure 5-10. Executing sensor.py application

It initializes smbus by calling smbus.SMBus(1). Then, it defines the I2C address of the PCF8591 AD/DA converter module with 0x48:

```
bus = smbus.SMBus(1)
address = 0x48
```

Next, the program defines three functions—photo(), potentiometer(), and thermistor()—to read sensor data. It uses the read_i2c_block_data() function to read the sensor data by passing the I2C address and channel data.

```python
def photo():
    val = bus.read_i2c_block_data(address,1,2)
    return val

def potentiometer():
    val = bus.read_i2c_block_data(address,3,2)
    return val

def thermistor():
    val = bus.read_i2c_block_data(address,0,2)
    return val
```

Now it uses try-catch to prevent errors. It implements infinite looping to call the preceding functions.

```python
try:
    while 1:
        # reading data

except KeyboardInterrupt:
    pass

print("done")
```

Inside the while-looping, it calls the three functions. The result of the sensor reading is printed to Terminal using the print() function.

```python
val = thermistor()
print('thermistor: ',val[1])
time.sleep(1)

val = photo()
print('photo: ',val[1])
time.sleep(1)

val = potentiometer()
```

```
print('potentiometer: ',val[1])
time.sleep(1)
```

Actuator Programming

In this section, you will write a program to interact with the actuator device. For this simple demo, you will use an LED to control the LED brightness. You will set the LED brightness from 0 to 100.

Use the PWM pin to set the brightness value. First, connect an LED to pin 33. Next, write a Python program to access the GPIO.

Open your Python editor. Then, write this complete program as follows:

```
import Jetson.GPIO as GPIO
import time

output_pin = 33 # PWM
GPIO.setmode(GPIO.BOARD)
GPIO.setup(output_pin, GPIO.OUT, initial=GPIO.HIGH)
pwm = GPIO.PWM(output_pin, 50)

val = 25
incr = 5
print("brightness: ", val)
pwm.start(val)
try:
    while 1:
        time.sleep(1)
        if val >= 100:
            incr = -incr
        if val <= 0:
            incr = -incr
```

```
        val += incr
        print("brightness: ", val)
        pwm.ChangeDutyCycle(val)

except KeyboardInterrupt:
    pwm.stop()
    GPIO.cleanup()

print("done")
```

Save this program as *actuator.py*. Now you can run this program on your NVIDIA Jetson Nano. You can open Terminal and navigate to the directory where the *actuator.py* file is placed. Type the following command to execute the actuator program:

```
$ sudo python3 actuator.py
```

After execution, you should see the program output. Figure 5-11 shows my program output from the *actuator.py* application. You can also see LED brightness changes.

How does it work?

First, it imports all required libraries into the program.

```
import Jetson.GPIO as GPIO
import time
```

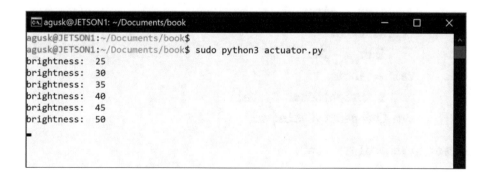

Figure 5-11. *Brightness application*

It declares the PWM pin and configures this pin to the Jetson.GPIO module. It uses GPIO.PWM for PWM implementation.

```
output_pin = 33 # PWM
GPIO.setmode(GPIO.BOARD)
GPIO.setup(output_pin, GPIO.OUT, initial=GPIO.HIGH)
pwm = GPIO.PWM(output_pin, 50)
```

Next, it initializes the brightness value to 25. Then, it starts to run PWM by calling the start() function.

```
val = 25
incr = 5
print("brightness: ", val)
pwm.start(val)
```

Last, it performs infinite-looping. It sets the LED brightness using the ChangeDutyCycle() function. If use breaks the looping, the program stops the PWM process by calling pwm.stop(). It also clears GPIO resources by calling the GPIO.cleanup() function.

```
try:
    while 1:
        time.sleep(1)
        if val >= 100:
            incr = -incr
        if val <= 0:
            incr = -incr
        val += incr
        print("brightness: ", val)
        pwm.ChangeDutyCycle(val)

except KeyboardInterrupt:
    pwm.stop()
```

```
    GPIO.cleanup()
print("done")
```

Summary

We have learned how to set up GPIO on the NVIDIA Jetson Nano. We also developed programs to implement sensor and actuator programs. We used the I2C protocol to communicate with sensor devices.

Next, we will learn how to work a camera on the NVIDIA Jetson Nano. We will use the CSI camera module.

CHAPTER 6

NVIDIA Jetson Nano Camera

We can use a camera with the NVIDIA Jetson Nano board. Then, we can make a smart device-based NVIDIA Jetson Nano. In this chapter, we will explore how to access a camera module from the NVIDIA Jetson Nano board and how to attach that camera module. Then, we will install the *OpenCV* library on the NVIDIA Jetson Nano. Finally, we will develop programs to take pictures and record video.

You will learn about the following topics in this chapter:

- Setting up a camera module

- Testing the camera

- Installing the *OpenCV* library

- Show video streaming from camera

- Taking a picture with the camera

- Recording video

Make sure you have a USB camera or/and camera CSI to implement all demos in this chapter.

© Agus Kurniawan 2021
A. Kurniawan, *IoT Projects with NVIDIA Jetson Nano*,
https://doi.org/10.1007/978-1-4842-6452-2_6

Introduction

The NVIDIA Jetson Nano is an Internet of Things (IoT) solution to address your problems for IoT or general purposes. You can attach a camera to the NVIDIA Jetson Nano board. You can build programs such as computer vision or intelligence vision. By applying machine learning libraries on the NVIDIA Jetson Nano, you can make a smart device.

In this chapter, we will explore how to work with a camera on the NVIDIA Jetson Nano board. You can then create Python programs to access the camera from the NVIDIA Jetson Nano.

Camera Interfaces and Modules

Technically, you can attach the camera module over the CSI interface or via USB. If you have the NVIDIA Jetson Nano A02 model, you will have one camera CSI interface. For the NVIDIA Jetson Nano B01 model, you will have two camera CSI interfaces. Figure 6-1 shows the camera CSI interface.

Figure 6-1. *Camera CSI interface on NVIDIA Jetson Nano*

You can get a camera CSI module at your local or online electronic store. You also can use the Raspberry Pi Camera v2. You can buy this module at https://www.raspberrypi.org/products/camera-module-v2/. There is also the Raspberry Pi NoIR camera, which you can see in Figure 6-2.

Figure 6-2. *Raspberry Pi Camera v2 (image from seeedstudio. com)*

You can also use a USB camera, such as a webcam. The NVIDIA Jetson Nano has four USB interfaces, so you can attach a USB camera to one of the board USB interfaces.

Set Up Camera Module

To set up the camera, just attach it to the camera interface on the board. For instance, if you have a camera CSI, you can put it on the CSI interface on the NVIDIA Jetson Nano. You can see my camera CSI in Figure 6-3. Otherwise, you can use a USB camera and attach it to the USB interface of the NVIDIA Jetson Nano.

Figure 6-3. *Attaching Raspberry Pi NoIR camera to NVIDIA Jetson Nano*

After attaching the camera to the NVIDIA Jetson Nano, verify it using this command:

```
$ ls /dev/video*
```

You should see your attached camera. For instance, I attached camera CSI and USB camera devices so you can see my program output in Figure 6-4.

Figure 6-4. *Checking attached camera devices*

Once you have attached your camera module, test it. For camera CSI, you can use the nvarguscamerasrc command. You can learn how to use the camera CSI with the nvarguscamerasrc command at https://github. com/JetsonHacksNano/CSI-Camera.

First, specify which camera CSI will be used. For the NVIDIA Jetson Nano A02 model, only use 0 for single camera, but if you have the NVIDIA Jetson Nano B01 model, you can select camera 0 or 1. For instance, if you attach a camera CSI to CSI interface 0, you can type this command:

```
$ nvarguscamerasrc sensor_id=0
```

Then, you can show the camera using nvarguscamerasrc. You can type this command:

```
$ gst-launch-1.0 nvarguscamerasrc sensor_id=0 ! \
    'video/x-raw(memory:NVMM),width=3280, height=2464,
    framerate=21/1, format=NV12' ! \
    nvvidconv flip-method=0 ! 'video/x-raw,width=960,
    height=720' ! \
    nvvidconv ! nvegltransform ! nveglglessink -e
```

Change sensor_id=0 to sensor_id=1 if you connect a camera CSI to CSI interface 2. Then, press *Enter*. You should see a dialog that shows the video from the camera CSI. You can see my program output in Figure 6-5.

Install OpenCV for Python3s

You can create a Python program with which to access the camera on your NVIDIA Jetson Nano. Use the *OpenCV* library to work with the camera. Technically, you can install *OpenCV* using this command:

```
$ sudo apt-get install python3-opencv
```

If you want to install the latest version of *OpenCV*, you can follow the installation instructions here: https://github.com/jkjung-avt/jetson_nano. First, increase the NVIDIA Jetson Nano's memory by increasing swap memory. You can type this command:

```
$ sudo nvpmodel -m 0
$ sudo jetson_clocks
```

Figure 6-5. *Displaying a live video from camera*

Now you can install *OpenCV*. You can run one of the *install_opencv-*. sh* files. For instance, if you want to install *OpenCV 3.4.8*, you can type these commands:

```
$ git clone https://github.com/jkjung-avt/jetson_nano
$ cd jetson_nano
$ ./install_opencv-3.4.8.sh
```

It will take several minutes. After installation is complete, verify the *OpenCV* version by using Python. You can type these commands:

```
$ python3
>>> import cv2
>>> cv2.__version__
```

You should see the *OpenCV* version in Terminal. Otherwise, you probably will get errors upon installation. Next, you can build Python programs to access the camera CSI and USB camera.

Displaying Live Video

In this section, you will develop two Python programs to show live video from the camera. The first program uses a camera USB, and the second program uses a camera CSI. After that, you will implement these programs using Python.

Displaying Video with USB Camera

You use *OpenCV* to show live video from the USB camera. To access the camera, use VideoCapture() and pass in the video number. You already have the video ID from Figure 6-4. In my case, I have a USB camera on /dev/video1 so I pass value 1 to VideoCapture().

After you obtain the VideoCapture object, you can read streaming video using the read() function. To show video streaming, you can use imshow() from *OpenCV*.

For implementation, create a Python file called *camera-usb-demo.py*. Write this complete program:

```python
import numpy as np
import cv2

# change camera no
cap = cv2.VideoCapture(1)

while(True):
    ret, frame = cap.read()
    cv2.imshow('frame',frame)
    if cv2.waitKey(1) & 0xFF == ord('q'):
        break

cap.release()
cv2.destroyAllWindows()
```

This program will run continuously until you press the *Q* key. To run this program, you can type this command in Terminal:

```
$ sudo python3 camera-usb-demo.py
```

You should see a dialog that is showing live video from a camera. Figure 6-6 shows the video stream on my NVIDIA Jetson Nano desktop. To close a program, press the *Q* key.

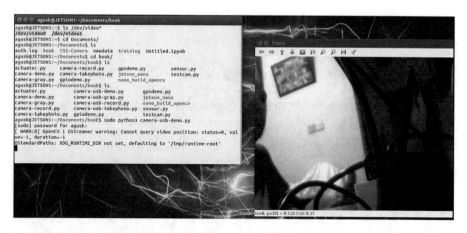

Figure 6-6. *Program output for camera-usb-demo.py*

You can see that the live video from the *camera-usb-demo.py* program is in full color. You also can make video stream in grayscale. When you have an image from `cv2.read()`, you can convert it to grayscale using the `cv2.cvtColor()` function. You can modify the *camera-usb-demo.py* program as follows:

```
import numpy as np
import cv2

cap = cv2.VideoCapture(1)

while(True):
    ret, frame = cap.read()

    gray = cv2.cvtColor(frame, cv2.COLOR_BGR2GRAY)
            cv2.imshow('frame',gray)
    if cv2.waitKey(1) & 0xFF == ord('q'):
        break

cap.release()
cv2.destroyAllWindows()
```

Save this program as *camera-usb-gray.py*. Then, you can run this program by typing this command:

```
$ sudo python3 camera-usb-gray.py
```

Now you should see live video in grayscale. You can see my program output in Figure 6-7.

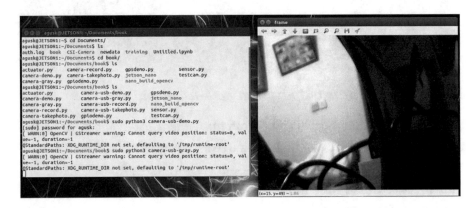

Figure 6-7. *Program output for camera-usb-gray.py*

Displaying Video with Camera CSI

You cannot read video from a camera CSI using `cv2.VideoCapture()`. You should stream video with `cvs2.CAP_GSTREAMER`. Then, you should retrieve the video using `nvarguscamerasrc`.

In this section, you will build a Python program to display live video from your camera CSI. Create a function, `gstreamer_pipeline()`, to retrieve the streaming video. Then, pass this function to `cv2.VideoCapture()`.

For testing, create a Python file, *camera-csi-demo.py*. Then, declare the `gstreamer_pipeline()` function as follows:

```
import numpy as np
import cv2
```

```
def gstreamer_pipeline(
    capture_width=640,
    capture_height=480,
    display_width=640,
    display_height=480,
    framerate=21,
    flip_method=0,
):
    return (
        "nvarguscamerasrc! "
        "video/x-raw(memory:NVMM), "
        "width=(int)%d, height=(int)%d, "
        "format=(string)NV12, framerate=(fraction)%d/1 ! "
        "nvvidconv flip-method=%d ! "
        "video/x-raw, width=(int)%d, height=(int)%d,
        format=(string)BGRx ! "
        "videoconvert ! "
        "video/x-raw, format=(string)BGR ! appsink"
        % (
            capture_width,
            capture_height,
            framerate,
            flip_method,
            display_width,
            display_height,
        )
    )
```

Now, call cv2.VideoCapture() and pass gstreamer_pipeline()
into the VideoCapture() object. Also set cv2.CAP_GSTREAMER to cv2.
VideoCapture(). Next, display a dialog to show live video using cv2.
imshow(). The following is the program implementation:

```
cap = cv2.VideoCapture(gstreamer_pipeline(flip_method=0), cv2.
CAP_GSTREAMER)
if cap.isOpened():
    indow_handle = cv2.namedWindow("CSI Camera", cv2.WINDOW_
    AUTOSIZE)
    while cv2.getWindowProperty("CSI Camera", 0) >= 0:
        ret, frame = cap.read()

        cv2.imshow('CSI Camera',frame)
        if cv2.waitKey(1) & 0xFF == ord('q'):
            break
else:
    print('Cannot open camera')

cap.release()
cv2.destroyAllWindows()
```

Save this program. You can run it using this command in NVIDIA
Jetson Nano's Terminal:

```
$ sudo python3 camera-csi-demo.py
```

After execution, you should see a dialog that is showing live video from the
camera CSI. Figure 6-8 shows my program output from *camera-csi-demo.py*.

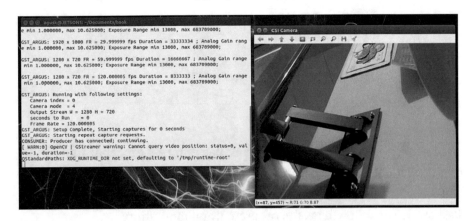

Figure 6-8. *Program output for camera-csi-demo.py*

Taking a Picture

In this demo, you will take a photo with the camera. You will develop two Python programs. The first program uses the camera USB, and the second program uses the camera CSI. Next, you will implement these programs using Python.

Taking a Picture with Camera USB

To take a picture from the camera USB, you can use the cv2.imwrite() function to save a video frame into a file. You can call this after the user presses the Q key. Then, you save a video frame into a file and close the application.

For this demo, you can modify a program from *camera-usb-demo. py*. Add codes for after the user presses the Q key. The following is a completed program for taking a picture from a camera USB:

```python
import numpy as np
import cv2

cap = cv2.VideoCapture(1)

while(True):
    ret, frame = cap.read()
    cv2.imshow('frame',frame)
    if cv2.waitKey(1) & 0xFF == ord('q'):
        cv2.imwrite('mypicture.png',frame)
        break

cap.release()
cv2.destroyAllWindows()
```

Save this program as *camera-usb-takephoto.py*. You can run it using this command in the NVIDIA Jetson Nano Terminal:

```
$ sudo python3 camera-usb-takephoto.py
```

After execution, you should see a dialog that is showing live video from the USB camera. Then, press the *Q* key to close the program. You should then see a file, *mypicture.png*.

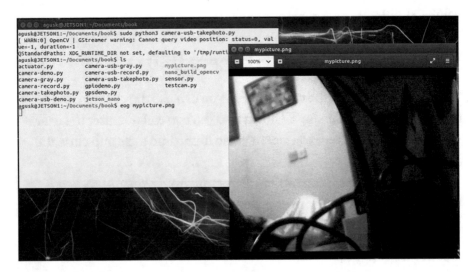

Figure 6-9. *Program output for camera-usb-takephoto.py with opening a photo file*

You can open this picture file using this command:

```
$ eog mypicture.png
```

You should have a dialog displaying the *mypicture.png* file. Figure 6-9 shows my program output with the *mypicture.png* file, a result of taking a picture with the USB camera.

Taking a Picture with Camera CSI

You can take a picture from a camera CSI using cv2.imwrite(). Since you are using a camera CSI, use the gstreamer_pipeline() function to obtain live video.

You can modify the *camera-usb-takephoto.py* program. Use gstreamer_pipeline() to pass to the cv2.VideoCapture() function. Now, you can create a new file, *camera-csi-takephoto.py*. This program is modified from the *camera-usb-takephoto.py* file.

```
import numpy as np
import cv2

def gstreamer_pipeline..
..
..

cap = cv2.VideoCapture(gstreamer_pipeline(flip_method=0), cv2.
CAP_GSTREAMER)
if cap.isOpened():
    indow_handle = cv2.namedWindow("CSI Camera", cv2.WINDOW_
    AUTOSIZE)
    while cv2.getWindowProperty("CSI Camera", 0) >= 0:
        ret, frame = cap.read()

        cv2.imshow('CSI Camera',frame)
        if cv2.waitKey(1) & 0xFF == ord('q'):
            cv2.imwrite('mypicture-csi.png',frame)
            break
else:
    print('Cannot open camera')

cap.release()
cv2.destroyAllWindows()
```

Save this program. You can run it using this command in the NVIDIA Jetson Nano Terminal:

```
$ sudo python3 camera-csi-takephoto.py
```

After execution, you should see a dialog that is showing live video from the camera CSI. Then, press the *Q* key to close the program. You should see a file, *mypicture-csi.png*.

Figure 6-10. *Program output for camera-csi-takephoto.py with opening a photo file*

You can open this picture file using this command:

```
$ eog mypicture-csi.png
```

You should have a dialog displaying the *mypicture-csi.png* file. Figure 6-10 shows my program output with the *mypicture.png* file, a result of taking a picture with the USB camera.

Recoding Video

In this section, you will record a video with the camera into an AVI file. First, implement the USB camera. You can create a Python file called *camera-usb-reord.py*. For instance, my USB camera is detected as /dev/ video1. Declare your VideoCapture as follows:

```
import numpy as np
import cv2

cap = cv2.VideoCapture(1)
```

Then, obtain the frame width and height from the VideoCapture object using the cap.get() function:

```
w=int(cap.get(cv2.CAP_PROP_FRAME_WIDTH ))
h=int(cap.get(cv2.CAP_PROP_FRAME_HEIGHT ))
```

Define a VideoWriter object to write streaming video into a file. I use the XVID video format as follows:

```
fourcc = cv2.VideoWriter_fourcc(*'XVID')
out = cv2.VideoWriter('output.avi',fourcc, 20.0, (w,h))
```

Now, perform a looping. You have a frame from cap.read(). Then, write this frame into a file using out.write():

```
while(cap.isOpened()):
    ret, frame = cap.read()
    if ret==True:
        out.write(frame)
        cv2.imshow('frame',frame)

        if cv2.waitKey(1) & 0xFF == ord('q'):
            break
    else:
```

```
        break

cap.release()
out.release()
cv2.destroyAllWindows()
```

Save this program as *camera-usb-record.py*. You can run it using this command in NVIDIA Jetson Nano's Terminal:

```
$ sudo python3 camera-usb-record.py
```

After execution, you should see a dialog that is showing live video from the USB camera. Then, press the *Q* key to close the program. You should see a video file, *output.avi*.

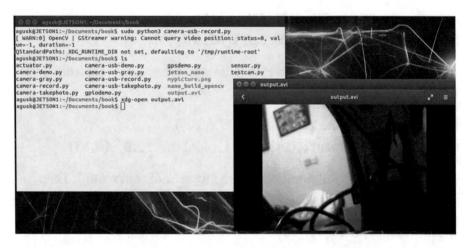

Figure 6-11. *Program output for camera-usb-record.py with opening a video file*

You can open this video file using this command:

```
$ xdg-open output.avi
```

You should have a dialog that is showing the video file. Figure 6-11 shows my program output from the *output.avi* file, a result of recording video from the USB camera.

Next, use the camera CSI to record video. You can modify *camera-usb-record.py* and use gstreamer_pipeline() to pass into VideoCapture object. The following is our program to record video from the camera CSI:

```
import numpy as np
import cv2

def gstreamer_pipeline(
...

...

cap = cv2.VideoCapture(gstreamer_pipeline(flip_method=0), cv2.
CAP_GSTREAMER)
if cap.isOpened():
    w=int(cap.get(cv2.CAP_PROP_FRAME_WIDTH ))
    h=int(cap.get(cv2.CAP_PROP_FRAME_HEIGHT ))

    fourcc = cv2.VideoWriter_fourcc(*'XVID')
    out = cv2.VideoWriter('output-csi.avi',fourcc, 20.0, (w,h))

    indow_handle = cv2.namedWindow("CSI Camera", cv2.WINDOW_
    AUTOSIZE)
    while cv2.getWindowProperty("CSI Camera", 0) >= 0:
        ret, frame = cap.read()

        cv2.imshow('CSI Camera',frame)
        out.write(frame)
        if cv2.waitKey(1) & 0xFF == ord('q'):
            break
else:
    print('Cannot open camera')
```

```
cap.release()
cv2.destroyAllWindows()
```

Save this program as *camera-csi-record.py*. You can run it using this command in the NVIDIA Jetson Nano terminal:

```
$ sudo python3 camera-csi-record.py
```

After execution, you should see a dialog that is showing live video from the camera CSI. Then, press the *Q* key to close the program. You should see a video file, *output.avi*.

You can open this video file using this command:

```
$ xdg-open output-csi.avi
```

You should have a dialog that is showing the video file. Figure 6-12 shows my program output from the *output.avi* file, a result of recording video from the camera CSI.

Figure 6-12. *Program output for camera-csi-record.py with opening a video file*

This is the end of the chapter. Do more practice demos to work with camera devices on the NVIDIA Jetson Nano.

Summary

We have learned how to use a camera on the NVIDIA Jetson Nano. We started by setting up the camera. Then, we created programs to display live video, take a picture, and record video.

Next, we will learn how to build deep-learning computations.

CHAPTER 7

Deep-Learning Computation

The NVIDIA Jetson Nano is designed to build smart applications. With a GPU with 128 cores, the NVIDIA Jetson Nano can be used to perform machine learning computations. In this chapter, we will work with the *Jetson Inference* library.

You will learn about the following topics in this chapter:

- Setting up *Jetson Inference* library

- Performing classification

- Performing live video from camera CSI

- Locating objects with DetectNet

Introduction

The NVIDIA Jetson Nano can be used for machine learning computations. Some Python libraries are also available for the GPU. In this chapter, we will explore the Hello API with the *Jetson Inference* library to build machine learning applications.

The *Jetson Inference* library is built based on deep-learning algorithms. It's written in C++ and with an exposed Python binding so you can build Python programs with it.

© Agus Kurniawan 2021
A. Kurniawan, *IoT Projects with NVIDIA Jetson Nano*,
https://doi.org/10.1007/978-1-4842-6452-2_7

Next, we will set up the *Jetson Inference* library on the NVIDIA Jetson Nano. Make sure your board is connected to the *internet*.

Setting Up Jetson Inference Library

Jetson Inference is used for AI library–based deep-learning computations. This library is written in C++ but is also available for Python binding. You can create Python programs using *Jetson Inference*.

You can read more about the *Jetson Inference* library at `https://github.com/dusty-nv/jetson-inference`. Before you set up this library, you need to install all required libraries. You can type these commands in the Terminal of the NVIDIA Jetson Nano:

```
$ sudo apt-get update
$ sudo apt-get install git cmake
$ sudo apt-get install libpython3-dev python3-numpy
```

Next, build the *Jetson Inference* library from the source code. Clone *Jetson Inference* from GitHub. After that, build the library. You can type these commands to clone and build the library:

```
$ git clone https://github.com/dusty-nv/jetson-inference
$ cd jetson-inference
$ git submodule update --init
$ mkdir build
$ cd build
$ cmake ../
```

During this installation process, you will see a dialog as shown in Figure 7-1. Select some models that you want to use in applications. Make sure your NVIDIA Jetson Nano storage is available. You also will be asked to install PyTorch, as shown in Figure 7-2. Select PyTorch for your Python version.

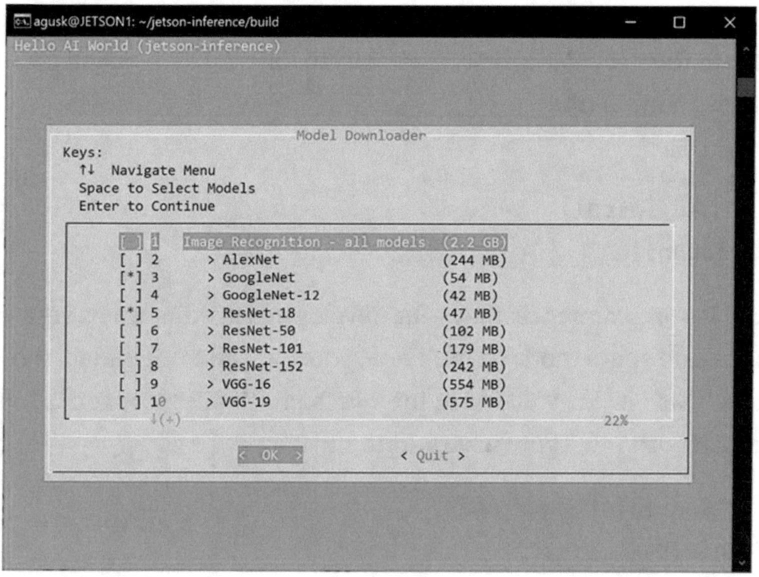

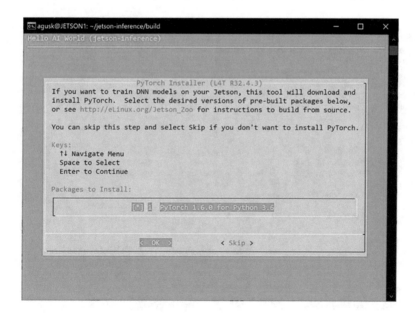

Figure 7-1. *Select model for training data*

Figure 7-2. *Installing PyTorch for Python*

This process takes several minutes to complete. After it is finished, navigate to the <jetson-inference>/build folder. Then, install this library using these commands:

```
$ make
$ sudo make install
$ sudo ldconfig
```

Now *Jetson Inference* is ready for development. Sometimes you want to modify or add some model data. Then, you can call a download-models program. This tool is available in the <jetson-inference>/tools folder, as shown in Figure 7-3. Type these commands:

```
$ cd jetson-inference/tools
$ ./download-models.sh
```

After that, you will see the dialog shown in Figure 7-3. You can select some model data for testing. This tool will download them directly.

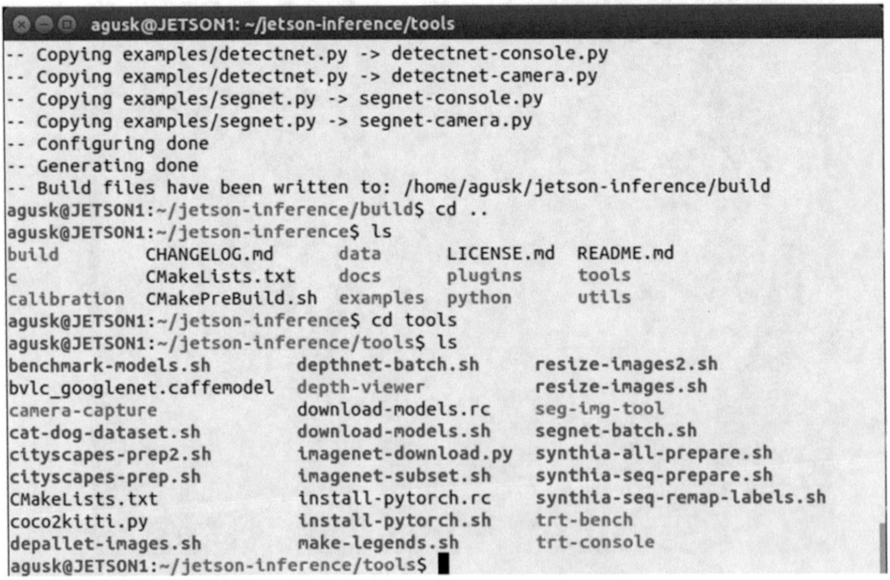

Figure 7-3. *Program tools on Jetson Inferences*

Data Classification

In this section, you will explore some program samples from the *Jetson Inference* library. You will implement data classification using *my-recognition. py*, a program that can recognize object type based on a data model. This file is available in the <jetson-inference>python/examples folder.

To work with this program, you should download model data, such as googlenet. You can download this data using the *download-models.sh* tool, in Figure 7-1.

You can open the *my-recognition.py* file, and then you will have the following completed codes:

```
import jetson.inference
import jetson.utils

import argparse


# parse the command line
parser = argparse.ArgumentParser()
parser.add_argument("filename", type=str, help="filename of the
image to process")
parser.add_argument("--network", type=str, default="googlenet",
help="model to use, can be:  googlenet, resnet-18, ect.")
opt = parser.parse_args()

# load an image (into shared CPU/GPU memory)
img = jetson.utils.loadImage(opt.filename)

# load the recognition network
net = jetson.inference.imageNet(opt.network)

# classify the image
class_idx, confidence = net.Classify(img)

# find the object description
```

```
class_desc = net.GetClassDesc(class_idx)
```

```
# print out the result
print("image is recognized as '{:s}' (class #{:d}) with {:f}%
confidence".format(class_desc, class_idx, confidence * 100))
```

For this demo, use the image file *black_bear.jpg* from the <jetson-inference>/examples/my-recognition folder. Copy this file into the <jetson-inference>python/examples folder. Navigate to the <jetson-inference>python/examples folder and run this program by typing this command:

```
$ sudo python3 my-recognition.py black_bear.jpg
```

When you run this for the first time, it takes several minutes because this application will perform the training process. This program performs object detection, as shown in Figure 7-4.

How does it work?

```
● ● ◎   agusk@JETSON1: ~/jetson-inference/python/examples
[TRT]       binding 1
                 -- index    1
                 -- name     'prob'
                 -- type     FP32
                 -- in/out   OUTPUT
                 -- # dims   3
                 -- dim #0   1000 (SPATIAL)
                 -- dim #1   1 (SPATIAL)
                 -- dim #2   1 (SPATIAL)
[TRT]
[TRT]       binding to input 0 data   binding index:  0
[TRT]       binding to input 0 data   dims (b=1 c=3 h=224 w=224) size=602112
[TRT]       binding to output 0 prob   binding index:  1
[TRT]       binding to output 0 prob   dims (b=1 c=1000 h=1 w=1) size=4000
[TRT]
[TRT]       device GPU, /usr/local/bin/networks/bvlc_googlenet.caffemodel initializ
ed.
[TRT]       imageNet -- loaded 1000 class info entries
[TRT]       imageNet -- networks/bvlc_googlenet.caffemodel initialized.
class 0295 - 0.989746  (American black bear, black bear, Ursus americanus, Euarc
tos americanus)
image is recognized as 'American black bear, black bear, Ursus americanus, Euarc
tos americanus' (class #295) with 98.974609% confidence
agusk@JETSON1:~/jetson-inference/python/examples$ ▮
```

Figure 7-4. *Output program from my-recognition.py*

First, load all required libraries. Also, prepare for input parameters from the user:

```
import jetson.inference
import jetson.utils

import argparse


# parse the command line
parser = argparse.ArgumentParser()
parser.add_argument("filename", type=str, help="filename of the
image to process")
parser.add_argument("--network", type=str, default="googlenet",
help="model to use, can be:  googlenet, resnet-18, ect.")
opt = parser.parse_args()
```

Pass the image file from the parameter into the loadImage() function. Then, load imageNet from the input parameter. If the user does not enter input, set googlenet for the imageNext() parameter.

```
# load an image (into shared CPU/GPU memory)
img = jetson.utils.loadImage(opt.filename)

# load the recognition network
net = jetson.inference.imageNet(opt.network)
```

Now you'll perform a classification process using the net. Classify() function. You also obtain the object description by calling the GetClassDesc() function.

```
# classify the image
class_idx, confidence = net.Classify(img)

# find the object description
class_desc = net.GetClassDesc(class_idx)
```

Last, print the result of the classification in Terminal. You will print values such as class_idx, class_desc, and confidence.

```
print("image is recognized as '{:s}' (class #{:d}) with {:f}%
confidence".format(class_desc, class_idx, confidence * 100))
```

Now do more practice exercises by using some picture files to perform the classification process.

Opening an Image File

You can open an image file using *Jetson Inference Utils*. You can call loadImageRGBA() to load an image file. Then, you display this picture using a glDisplay object. To render an image file to the monitor, call RenderOnce() from glDisplay.

For implementation, you can create a file called *jetson-image.py*. This program will open *black_bear.jpg*. You can copy this image file to the current folder of the *jetson-image.py* file. Now you can write this completed program from *jetson-image.py*:

```
import jetson.utils

img, width, height = jetson.utils.loadImageRGBA ("black_bear.
jpg")
display = jetson.utils.glDisplay()

while display.IsOpen():
    display.RenderOnce(img, width, height)
    display.SetTitle("{:s} | {:d}x{:d} | {:.1f} FPS".
format("Camera Viewer", width, height, display.GetFPS()))
```

Save this program. You can run it by typing this command:

```
$ sudo python3 jetson-image.py
```

After executing the program, you should see the image of *black_bear. jpg* on the monitor, as shown in Figure 7-5.

Figure 7-5. *Showing image file using Jetson Utils library*

Live Video from Camera CSI

You can show live video from a camera CSI using *Jetson Inference Utils*. You can use gstCamera() and pass the camera CSI's address. For instance, if your camera CSI is detected as /dev/video0, you can pass the value 0 to gstCamera(). Then, you can display the contents of the camera CSI to the glDisplay object.

To implement, create a file called *jetson-csi.py*. In this demo, my camera CSI is attached on /dev/video0, so I can write this complete program for jetson-csi.py as follows:

```
import jetson.utils

camera = jetson.utils.gstCamera(640,480,"0")
display = jetson.utils.glDisplay()

camera.Open()
while display.IsOpen():
        img, width, height = camera.CaptureRGBA()
        display.RenderOnce(img, width, height)
        display.SetTitle("{:s} | {:d}x{:d} | {:.1f} FPS".
format("Camera Viewer", width, height, display.GetFPS()))

camera.Close()
```

Save this program. You can run it by typing this command:

```
$ sudo python3 jetson-csi.py
```

After executing the program, you should see live video from your camera CSI.

Locating Objects with DetectNet

In this section, you will detect an object's location using the DetectNet object. You can use an image file as input, or streaming video. For this demo, use the *black_bear.jpg* file for testing.

Create a Python file called *jetson-image-detectnet.py*. You can write your program into this file. First, import all required libraries:

```
import jetson.inference
import jetson.utils
```

Then, load training data using detectNet(),passing in ssd-mobilenet-v2. After that, load *black_bear.jpg* by calling loadImageRGBA() and glDisplay objects.

```
net = jetson.inference.detectNet("ssd-mobilenet-v2",
threshold=0.5)
img, width, height = jetson.utils.loadImageRGBA ("black_bear.
jpg")
display = jetson.utils.glDisplay()
```

Now you can detect an image file using the Detect() function.

```
detections = net.Detect(img, width, height)
```

Next, display the result to monitor as follows:

```
display.RenderOnce(img, width, height)
display.SetTitle("{:s} | {:d}x{:d} | {:.1f} FPS".format("Camera
Viewer", width, height, display.GetFPS()))
```

```
# press ENTER to exit
input()
```

Save this program. You can run it by typing this command:

```
$ sudo python3 jetson-image-detectnet.py
```

After executing the program, you should see the *black_bear.jpg* file with object detection location, as shown in Figure 7-6.

Figure 7-6. *Locating objects*

If you want to use a camera CSI as the input to DetectNet, you can use gstCamera(). Then, object the image frame from the camera. You can write this completed program for the object:

```
import jetson.inference
import jetson.utils

net = jetson.inference.detectNet("ssd-mobilenet-v2",
threshold=0.5)
camera = jetson.utils.gstCamera(640,480,"0")
display = jetson.utils.glDisplay()

camera.Open()
```

```
while display.IsOpen():
    img, width, height = camera.CaptureRGBA()
    detections = net.Detect(img, width, height)
    display.RenderOnce(img, width, height)
    display.SetTitle("{:s} | {:d}x{:d} | {:.1f} FPS".
format("Camera Viewer", width, height, display.GetFPS()))

camera.Close()
```

Save this program as *jetson-csi-detectnet.py*. Now you can run it by typing this command:

```
$ sudo python3 jetson-csi-detectnet.py
```

After having executed the program, you should see live video from the camera CSI along with object-detection location.

This is the end of this chapter. You can practice implementing the *Jetson Inference* library in your own projects.

Summary

We have learned how to work the *Jetson Inference* library to perform deep learning computations on the NVIDIA Jetson Nano board. We also accessed camera CSI using *Jetson Inference Utils*. Next, we performed object classification and object detection location.

Index

A, B

adduser command, 31
Appearance tool, 23

C

Camera
    displaying live video, 91
        CSI, 94–96
        USB camera, 91–94
    interface/modules, 86, 87
    OpenCV, Python3s, 90, 91
    recording video, 101–104
    setup module, 88, 89
    taking picture
        CSI, 99, 100
        USB, 97, 98
cap.get() function, 101
C/C++, 54–57
cv2.imwrite()function, 97
cv2.VideoCapture(), 95, 99

D

Deep learning computations
    camera CSI, 115
    data classification, 111–114
    DetectNet object, 116, 118
    Jetson Inference, 108, 110
    open image file, 114, 115
Desktop personalization, 22, 23

E, F

Editor tools, 50–54

G

General-purpose input/output
    (GPIO)
    actuator programming, 80–83
    definition, 64
    pins, 65, 66
    programming, 68–73
    sensor programming, 73–79
    setting up, 66, 68
GPIO.BOARD model, 72
GPIO.output() function, 72
gstreamer_pipeline()
    function, 94, 99

H

Hardware preparation, 8, 9

© Agus Kurniawan 2021
A. Kurniawan, *IoT Projects with NVIDIA Jetson Nano*,
https://doi.org/10.1007/978-1-4842-6452-2

Printed in the United States
By Bookmasters